President Grant Reconsidered

President Grant Reconsidered

Frank J. Scaturro

MADISON BOOKS
Lanham • New York • Oxford

Published by Madison Books
4720 Boston Way
Lanham, Maryland 20706

12 Hid's Copse Road
Cumnor Hill, Oxford OX2 9JJ, England

Distributed by National Book Network

Library of Congress Cataloging-in-Publication Data

Scaturro, Frank J.
    President Grant reconsidered / Frank J. Scaturro.
       p.   cm.
    Originally published: Lanham : University Press of America, 1998.
    Includes bibliographical references and index.
    ISBN 1-56833-132-0 (alk. paper)
    1. Grant, Ulysses S. (Ulysses Simpson), 1822–1885. 2. United States—
Politics and government—1869–1877.   3. Presidents—United States Biography.
I. Title.
    [E671.S32   1999]
    973.8'2'092—dc21
    [B]   99–36093
                                                                        CIP

⊖™ The paper used in this publication meets the minimum requirements of
American National Standard for Information Sciences—Permanence of
Paper for Printed Library Materials, ANSI/NISO Z39.48–1992.
Manufactured in the United States of America.

President Grant, c. 1869

Courtesy Missouri Historical Society, St. Louis

*This book is dedicated to
the people of the United
States, and to others in the
free world who share in
the legacies of worthy
American presidents.*

CONTENTS

PREFACE

One reviewer of a biography about Ulysses S. Grant wrote in 1917, "One takes up each new biography of Grant with the sort of interest with which a physician receives a new treatise on cancer. He is a problem, as yet unsolved, which will probably be solved, and each unread attempt may contain the solution."[1] However enigmatic a historical subject Grant's life generally has been, it is his presidency that epitomizes the puzzle, and this enigma remains just as strong today as it was eighty years ago.

It is with a certain sense of discouragement that I have written this reassessment of Grant's presidency for public consumption, because I believe that attitudes and assumptions that have been fixed in history books for so many decades are very difficult to overcome, no matter how wrong I believe them to be.

Our citizens are taught from early grade school to revere George Washington and Abraham Lincoln as great presidents, and not long afterwards, they may briefly encounter President Ulysses S. Grant, who still almost invariably is viewed on the opposite end of the spectrum. After my own study of American history, I do not think it seriously can be maintained that historians approach Grant with the same predisposition they bring to examinations of other presidents.

I generally agree with the final verdicts on Washington and Lincoln (although I do not believe their claim to greatness is as exclusive as many seem to think), but in other areas, history has been terribly distorted by the biases of those who write it—or of the sources to which well-meaning writers refer. I have chosen President Grant as my subject because I am particularly interested in presidential history and believe that the dominant interpretations of his presidency stand collectively as the most inaccurate component of this area of history.

---

[1] Fish, p. 885.

As compared to a chronological or definitive account of Grant's presidency, this study devotes disproportionate attention to the corruption and Reconstruction issues because I believe the most distortion arises from misunderstandings of these two subjects. The fourth chapter, which covers Grant's other presidential achievements, is too short to do the subject justice. A study that sought to provide simply an account of the Grant administration without adding emphasis to certain issues in order to remedy past distortions would devote more space to the issues that that chapter covers.

I may seem too idealistic in clinging to the belief that there is in fact "pure" history behind much of what history books have distorted, but I hope the reader will accept this as an honest attempt to uncover a chapter of history that has been buried too deep for too long.

FRANK SCATURRO

I

INTRODUCTION

In *The American Political Tradition*, Richard Hofstadter effectively summarizes historians' traditional verdict on the presidency of Ulysses S. Grant in twelve words: "not much need be said. Grant's administrations are notorious for their corruption."[2] At the time of his death in 1885, many considered Grant the "Second Father of His Country," and contemporaries placed him in the highest echelon of great Americans along with Washington and Lincoln. Circumstances, however, would forge a strikingly different image of Grant from that of his two legendary predecessors. "Grant was an ignorant and confused President," writes Thomas A. Bailey, "and his eight long years in blunderland are generally regarded as a national disgrace."[3]

In the twentieth century, the peacetime career of U.S. Grant, the principal author of Union victory during the Civil War, has been widely condemned. Historians have consistently ranked Grant among the worst presidents, and the Arthur Schlesinger polls of 1948 and 1962, as well as the Murray-Blessing poll of 1982, place him second to rockbottom Warren G. Harding among presidential "failures."[4] C. Vann Woodward declares that "the Administration of President Ulysses S. Grant. . . . stands for the all-time low point in statesmanship and political morality in our history."[5]

---

[2] Hofstadter, p. 223.
[3] Bailey, *Presidential Greatness*, p. 295.
[4] Murray and Blessing, pp. 16-17.
[5] C.V. Woodward, p. 53.

Grant's presidency nevertheless covers one of the most critical periods in American history. In fact, James D. Richardson, editor of *Messages and Papers of the Presidents* (1897), asserts that Grant was "a great President, who after Washington and Lincoln, was the Chief Magistrate during the most difficult period in our Nation's history."[6] The only president between Andrew Jackson and Woodrow Wilson (a period spanning 76 years) to serve two complete, consecutive terms, Grant indeed was in the White House during what most historians consider the last eight years of Reconstruction and the first eight years of the Gilded Age. In that respect, it was a very complex, checkered, almost schizophrenic presidency, which makes it particularly difficult to evaluate. While Grant was called upon to supply the steadiness, rectitude, and restraint of Washington, he also faced a social and political upheaval calling for radical measures reminiscent of Lincoln.

A study of this length cannot provide a thorough analysis of the entire Grant presidency. Rather, it will explore some historical trends, fundamental assumptions, and resulting judgments. Seeking possible loopholes and oversights in the traditional verdict on the Grant presidency, this study will attempt to establish the extent to which historians need to reconsider Grant as president. While it is important to mention each major facet of the Grant administration, special focus will be devoted to two issues—corruption and Reconstruction—as historical problems tied into historiographical difficulties that have been most central to historians' misunderstanding of the Grant presidency. The chapters in this account are thematically structured, but with the hope that the reader will never lose sight of the interconnectedness of all issues discussed, no matter how separate they initially might appear from each other. It is not until the extended analysis in the Reconstruction chapter and the subsequent conclusion that the issues of the preceding chapters are brought to full light and placed into perspective accordingly.

Considering the importance and complexity of Grant's years in the White House, it may seem strange that only one definitive study focuses solely on Grant's political career—William B. Hesseltine's *Ulysses S. Grant: Politician* (1935). Three other works attempt to discuss the Grant presidency in depth: Louis A. Coolidge's *Ulysses S. Grant* (1917), Allan Nevins' *Hamilton Fish: The Inner History of the Grant*

---

[6] Richardson VIII, p. 3956-D.

Administration (1936), and William S. McFeely's *Grant: A Biography* (1981).[7] All three, however, are too historiographically problematic to be accepted as final verdicts in themselves.

Coolidge's study, which concludes that in "constructive achievements . . . Grant's Administration ranks second only to that of Washington,"[8] has not been taken seriously by scholars. Nevins' study, though far lengthier than Hesseltine's, places its primary focus upon Secretary of State Fish. Nevins' reliance on Fish's diary gives rise to an unbalanced, naive account of the Grant presidency that too often provides little perspective beyond that of the Secretary of State and the author. It is doubtful that Fish himself would have endorsed Nevins' lopsided use of his sources to condemn almost every aspect of Grant's presidency besides Fish. Despite its length, the resulting study is too indirect to be considered definitive, and it seems to be premised on traditional bias against Grant without exploring the validity of that bias. McFeely's study has been criticized as the result of "sloppy research and problems of interpretation."[9] "Grant's contemporaries," asserts historian Brooks Simpson, "would have had a difficult time recognizing the man described in McFeely's book."[10] Indeed, McFeely himself is said to have commented that he viewed researching Grant's presidency as a "bore," and his contempt for Grant is apparent in the finished product.

Perhaps more importantly, Hesseltine, whose study is the most comprehensive of the four, makes a fundamental oversight on the issue of sources, the foundation upon which any solid history must rest. Asserting his "intention to reexamine Grant's political career impartially," Hesseltine insists that "[t]he task has been rendered difficult by the almost complete lack of Grant manuscripts. . . . [T]he

---

[7] While Adam Badeau's *Grant in Peace* (1887) contains valuable information, it is not listed with Hesseltine, Coolidge, Nevins, and McFeely because it discusses only a portion of the issues facing President Grant. Furthermore, Geoffrey Perret's *Ulysses S. Grant: Soldier and President* (1997), published after the completion (but before the publication) of the present work, does not warrant any revision of this analysis. While it does have strengths in other areas, Perret's book includes little focus on Grant's presidency, and much of that limited commentary consists of shallow, often irrelevant Gilded Age character sketches.

[8] Coolidge, p. 532.

[9] Simpson, letter.

[10] Simpson, "Butcher?," p. 83.

years of his presidency are singularly barren in documentary remains. Grant himself was a poor writer and had but a limited correspondence with his political associates."[11]   In 1962, twenty-seven years after Hesseltine's study, the Ulysses S. Grant Association began to amass a collection of over 200,000 Grant manuscripts, the vast majority of which were not published or otherwise available to scholars when Hesseltine wrote.   After publishing eighteen volumes of Grant's writings extending to the end of his military career, the Grant Association published volumes 19 and 20, covering only the first year and a half of his presidency, in 1995.   It has yet to publish the remaining presidential volumes, which will comprise by far the most definitive primary source on Grant's presidency.[12]   Without this crucial information, historians have been at a serious loss, and Hesseltine's glaring misjudgment in 1935 hints that a reconsideration based upon new sources is necessary for a truly definitive evaluation of Grant as president.

---

[11]   Hesseltine, p. vii.

[12]   Ulysses S. Grant Association brochures through 1995; Simon, pp. vii-viii.

II

GRANT THE MAN:
THE INTANGIBLE FACTOR

The existing consensus on the Grant presidency views the eighteenth president as a man whose naiveté and indifference to reform allowed the government to be torn apart by corruption. Before turning to corruption and other more concrete issues during the Grant era, any analysis of Grant's standing among historians should not neglect the less tangible, but still influential, role of the literary impressions of President Grant's personal character that dominate the thought of historians. Hesseltine, whose study best reflects the traditional historical consensus, does not question Grant's personal honesty but proceeds to portray him as "peculiarly ignorant of the Constitution and inept in handling men. His mental endowment was not great and he filled his state papers with platitudes rather than thoughts."[13] To Bailey, Grant "obviously lacked the mentality, adaptability, and interest to comprehend fully what was going on . . . much less to chart a farseeing and purposeful course."[14] "The popular idea of Grant has always been a depressing one," observes J.F.C. Fuller, "a leaden man of no great spirit, of no imagination and of little thought. . . . a man . . . utterly lacking in those qualities which give brilliance to human affairs."[15] Assertions of President Grant's limited mental capacity are so widespread, and they have been so casually accepted by the traditional consensus, that it would not be rash to conclude that historians have grown comfortable in expressing outright contempt for

---

[13] Hesseltine, p. viii.
[14] Bailey, *Presidential Greatness*, p. 138.
[15] Fuller, p. 58.

Grant. In *How They Became President: Thirty-Five Ways to the White House*, Rexford G. Tugwell asserts that "Grant's example is an encouraging one . . . . to those who lack the culture, the dignity, and even the minimum mental equipment necessary for the job. Almost anyone, it seems, can become President if the times are troubled."[16]

Such sentiments were shared by Grant's most bitter contemporary partisan critics, which raises the question of precisely what comprises the pool of information historians have been using for their studies of the Grant presidency. How is it that a president whose character was so widely admired in his own time later would be remembered as a blundering ignoramus, and how trustworthy is this assessment? Hesseltine himself provides part of the historiographical reason for Grant's low ranking as president, admitting that "many of the more persistent charges of Grant's stupidity and corruption were born in partisan politics and derive their validity from the political stump." What Grant's opponents left behind for historians is

> voluminous. Numbering in their ranks the New England literary group and the editors of some of the nation's most widely read newspapers, Grant's enemies were more literate than his friends. Consciously or unconsciously they stuffed the ballot boxes of history against Grant . . . .[17]

In his reassessment of Gilded Age politicians, Ari Hoogenboom asserts that the historian has exaggerated the period's corruption in part because of "the bias of his sources. The most articulate individuals in this age were its severest critics. Their enforced inactivity . . . gave them both a cause and the time for writing, while their enemies managed conventions and built railroads."[18] This invites an examination of Grant's enemies with a focus on their reliability, and a thorough look at the Grant presidency indicates that 1) Grant's contemporary Northern critics were, in a sense, the intellectual ancestors of later historians, and there is a serious issue of professional bias; and 2) there were many complex issues during his years in

---

[16] Tugwell, p. 232.
[17] Hesseltine, pp. vii-viii. See also Ari Hoogenboom, "Spoilsmen and Reformers: Civil Service Reform and Public Morality" in Morgan, pp. 71-72.
[18] Hoogenboom in Morgan, p. 71.

office—issues of such magnitude, in fact, that they call into question the role of the entire issue of corruption.

In his famous autobiography, *The Education of Henry Adams*, the author identified Grant as a type of man who "was pre-intellectual, archaic, and would have seemed so even to the cave-dwellers." For years, the discussion that followed has remained a source of entertainment for historians:

> Simple-minded beyond the experience of Wall Street or State Street, he resorted, like most men of the same intellectual calibre, to commonplaces when at a loss for expression . . . sometimes he made one doubt his good faith; as when he seriously remarked to a particularly bright young woman that Venice would be a fine city if it were drained. In Mark Twain, this suggestion would have taken rank among his best witticisms; in Grant it was a measure of simplicity not singular. . . . He had no right to exist. He should have been extinct for ages. The idea that, as society grew older, it grew one-sided, upset evolution, and made of education a fraud. That, two thousand years after Alexander the Great and Julius Caesar, a man like Grant should be called—and should actually and truly be—the highest product of the most advanced evolution, made evolution ludicrous. One must be as commonplace as Grant's own commonplaces to maintain such an absurdity. The progress of evolution from President Washington to President Grant, was alone evidence enough to upset Darwin.[19]

Of course, this passage was not written as a solid scholarly appraisal of Grant, but the fact that it has been the source of amusement for generations of historians betrays an unfortunate tendency toward contempt for a character that is not readily recognizable by preconceived notions of what type of personality merits respect. While Adams' words are not taken literally, his sentiment is shared widely, and several future historians, including Nevins, would point to Grant's remark about Venice as evidence of an inferior intellect.[20] "By the nature of things," Michael Les Benedict points out, "the journalists, litterateurs, and scholars who have written about Grant have been part of an intellectual community that has shared a set of expectations about how men of conscious intellect behave. When a man makes a great public reputation, one expects him to demonstrate an interest in public

---

[19] Adams, pp. 265-66.
[20] Nevins, p. 134.

events, to leave a record of his views and explanations of his actions. Grant disappoints such expectations. His leading characteristic was his taciturnity," a trait that historians have found little reason either to celebrate or to explore in order to discover the character that lies behind it.[21]

Through his career, Grant was known at various times as the "American Sphinx," "Ulysses the Silent," and the "Great Unspeakable."[22] "Any one could come into his presence . . . but only a few people could get at his thought," remarked one observer. "I have seen a man talk to Grant listening in rigid irresponse till, in sheer self-defense, the visitor was forced to rise and flee from the President's terrible accusing silence."[23] After a meeting with Grant, James A. Garfield noted in his diary, "His imperturbability is amazing. I am in doubt whether to call it greatness or stupidity."[24] This particular statement captures perfectly how enigmatic and elusive Grant's personality is, especially as a politician. Somehow, the historical consensus has succeeded at assembling an incongruent picture of the man in which imperturbability reflects the greatness of General Grant while that same quality reflects the stupidity of President Grant.

Actually, as Hamlin Garland writes, "he was in private a very social man."[25] General Horace Porter, Grant's aide de camp during the war and later his presidential secretary, asserted that "the exhibition of the remarkable power he possessed as a conversationalist was a revelation. I began to learn that his reputed reticence did not extend to his private intercourse, and that he had the ability to impart a peculiar charm to

---

[21] Benedict, p. 352. In the context of his generalship, this trait has been approached more sympathetically. For example, historians might take note of the following observation of Grant made by his aide de camp: "He would sit for hours in front of his tent, or just inside of it looking out, smoking a cigar very slowly, seldom with a paper or a map in his hands, and looking like the laziest man in camp. But at such periods his mind was working more actively than that of any one in the army. He talked less and thought more than any one in the service. . . . It was this quiet but intense thinking, and the well-matured ideas which resulted from it, that led to the prompt and vigorous action which was constantly witnessed during this year [1864], so pregnant with events." Porter, p. 250.

[22] Porter, p. 196.

[23] Garland, p. 400.

[24] Garfield III, p. 244.

[25] Garland, p. 402.

almost any topic."[26] John S. Wise "never found him" to be taciturn as president. "He always talked to me, and he always seemed to delight in putting questions as fast as he could ask them,"[27] a habit that remained from his school days.[28] Rutherford B. Hayes found that "after he warms up he is . . . cheerful, chatty, and good natured. . . . I feel just as much at ease with him as I do with intimate friends."[29] "You could walk with him for hours and he would not say a word," observed John Russell Young, the newspaper correspondent who followed Grant through his post-presidential trip around the world.

> And yet you might readily sit up with him until sunrise and never be permitted to say a word, because of his incessant, brilliant, penetrating conversation. It has been my privilege to meet some of the famous talkers of the day,—to stroll with Dickens, to rest under the spell of the exquisite power of Wendell Phillips, to listen to Bismarck over his pipe and caressing his hound,—but I never heard a more cogent, comprehensive talker than Grant.[30]

Frederick Douglass felt similarly: "Many who approached him told me he was a silent man. To me, he was one of the best conversationalists I have ever met."[31]

Grant's silence alone does not account for his criticism, however. More contempt tends to be expressed for the men who surrounded Grant than for the president himself. "Unable to respond with trust and warmth to the men of education, talent, and culture whose help he needed to make up for his own deficiencies," writes Woodward, "he turned a frozen face and steely armor toward them. Instead he found the companionship and warmth he craved in men of his own background, in his buddies of the war years, and in politicians on the make, as newly arrived as he was. They were often men of coarser grain and lower instincts than his own."[32] The emphasis historians traditionally place on Grant's alienation of "men of education and culture" is a curious phenomenon—one that is less definable than any

---

[26] Porter, pp. 29-30.
[27] Wise, p. 117.
[28] Garland, pp. 28-29.
[29] Benedict, p. 352.
[30] Young, *Men and Memories* II, p. 476.
[31] Benedict, p. 352.
[32] C.V. Woodward, p. 56.

matter of policy, but which has played no mean role in giving President Grant his present reputation. This phenomenon remains to be explored further.

A more careful look at Grant indicates a conscientious man with both a reluctance to enter the White House and a desire not to witness the sacrifice of the gains of Union victory that he had helped to secure during the Civil War. Distressed by the Reconstruction policy of Andrew Johnson, which opposed virtually every measure seeking to advance the rights of former slaves, Grant, finding himself in the middle of a political tug-of-war in the bitter battle between the president and Congress, displayed no behavior indicating presidential aspirations, but he did remain concerned about the fate of the country in the hands of what seemed a paralyzed national leadership. Contrary to the myth that he entered the presidency with no political experience, General-in-chief Grant was deeply involved in the national issues that were sweeping the country. He was frequently consulted during the preparation of Reconstruction legislation, and he essentially was charged by Congress with the responsibility of supervising Reconstruction's implementation.[33] His close friend, General William T. Sherman, wrote his father that Grant "does not want to be President, told me that 50 millions of dollars would not compensate him therefor, but that events might force him [in] spite of inclination . . . ."[34] Grant's "many good officers at the South," Sherman continued, "force him to the conclusion that there is necessary there some strong power to protect the negroes & union men against legal oppression, or the acts of badly disposed Ex-Rebels."[35]

Once in office, Grant maintained a close interest in the wide array of domestic and foreign policy issues that faced him, and he personally wrote most of his own messages.[36] While Grant was frequently accused by his enemies of being obtuse, his recorded observations on the issues of his day, many of which will be presented in this study, reflect a mind that was actually quite acute. His memory, which might have been photographic, was complemented by an ability to reduce a problem to

---

[33] Badeau, pp. 65, 72-73.
[34] Simpson, *Let Us Have Peace*, p. 214.
[35] Ibid., p. 215.
[36] Coolidge, p. 531; Porter, p. 7.

its basics and apply innovative solutions.[37] The side of his personality that revealed itself among intimates reflected a vast mental endowment that was combined with an ability to articulate. "Few men," wrote Hamilton Fish, "had more powers of conversation and of narration than he when in the company of intimate friends. . . . His memory was minute and accurate to a degree."[38] He combined an excellent memory for detail with unflinching honesty.[39] The notion that Grant was a poor writer, curiously advocated by Hesseltine, is rejected by the near-universal praise of Grant's *Personal Memoirs* as one of the greatest military autobiographies ever written, and George F. Hoar testified to Grant's "great readiness as a writer" while president, having seen "him write two messages to Congress, both of a good deal of importance, without pause or correction, and as rapidly as his pen could fly over the paper."[40] The messages, like so many others that Grant issued while president, were clear and concise, and they proved successful once they reached Congress.[41]

Supplementing his ability to perceive and to articulate was a deep compassion for the downtrodden, a trait that would lead to unpopular policies in two realms. "The typical Grant stereotype," writes Robert H. Keller, "can blind us to his humanity in Indian affairs,"[42] and the

---

[37] During the Civil War, Grant could remember the details of topography after a single look at a map, and as president, he "never forgot a face." Porter, pp. 66, 514; Garland, p. 398; Young, *Men and Memories* II, pp. 473-74.

[38] Nevins, pp. 134-35.

[39] Porter, pp. 75, 340-41. Porter recalls the following anecdote: "When he became President, an usher brought him a card one day while he was in a private room writing a message to Congress. 'Shall I tell the gentleman you are not in?' asked the usher. 'No,' answered the President; 'you will say nothing of the kind. I don't lie myself, and I won't have any one lie for me.'" Ibid., p. 341.

[40] Hoar I, p. 204. Porter makes a similar observation about Grant's writing during his generalship: "His work was performed swiftly and uninterruptedly, but without any marked display of nervous energy. His thoughts flowed as freely from his mind as the ink from his pen . . . ." Porter, p. 7. "[N]o matter how hurriedly he may write" his orders "on the field," commented General George G. Meade's chief of staff, "no one ever has the slightest doubt as to their meaning, or ever has to read them over a second time to understand them." Ibid., p. 241.

[41] Hoar I, pp. 204-06.

[42] Keller, p. 26.

same could be said about the several instances in which the president, visibly affected by reports of cruelty against blacks,[43] utilized troops in the South. Grant's messages condemning racial violence and defending political equality regardless of color remain a singular presidential demonstration of eloquence in the realm of civil rights in the nineteenth century.

It is unfortunate that accounts of his career tend to end at Appomattox, for Grant after 1865 would continue to make a significant mark on American history which largely remains a missing key to understanding both the full meaning of Union victory in the Civil War and the evolution of modern America. He also continued to grow as a man. Adam Badeau, Grant's military secretary, was abroad through most of his chief's presidency, and he met the former president in England, the first stop in his world trip, shortly after he left the White House. Badeau recorded how much Grant had grown since he last had seen him:

> . . . I noticed now a broader man in manner and character. He was far more conscious; he understood himself better; he knew his powers; he knew what he wanted to do and say under all circumstances. He was a greater man than the one I had left in America seven years before. I was especially struck with his poise . . . . No one had anticipated the great popular enthusiasm that welcomed him everywhere in England; but he was calm and undisturbed as of old . . . gratified deeply, but not elated. His fluency of speech amazed me. He had learned the art since I had met him last. . . . He remained as simple as ever in his bearing, and still almost plain, but he was seldom awkward or embarrassed now.[44]

That the dominant interpretation of Grant's character comes from the president's partisan critics almost to the exclusion of his more intimate associates suggests a serious obstacle to understanding a complex man who has been viewed even by contemporary intimates and biographers as an enigma. The mass of existing condemnatory literature displays a clear tendency to overlook the complexity of Grant's character in favor of a one-dimensional portrait, and it suggests to the careful eye not only that it is inaccurate, but also that its authors did not particularly care to do their subject justice. While it is important not to embrace blindly an interpretation of a president that is

---

[43] McFeely, p. 425.
[44] Badeau, pp. 178-79.

based solely on his own terms or on those of his friends, which rightfully would lead one to suspect a personality cult rather than true history, what has developed in Grant's case is the other extreme. The Grant administration retains a seemingly anti-intellectual character, and its peculiar historiography can be attributed to the extent to which President Grant alienated that portion of the nineteenth-century "intelligentsia" that comprised the intellectual ancestors of the twentieth-century American historical profession.

This study hopes to depart from tradition by taking Grant seriously as a president, but to do so challenges historians to transcend their own preconceptions about historical figures and public affairs. For years, Grant simply has been on a different wavelength from dominant modes of historical thought. Such is the case with most presidents who are rated as below standard, but when it comes to evaluating the Grant administration, historians have neglected to use all of their intuitive tools: it will be seen not only that President Grant had a vision for the country, but also that his still largely unknown views actually correspond remarkably to widely accepted ideas about American democracy.

III

THE REFORMERS AND THE CORRUPTION QUESTION

Although President Grant faced a wide array of critical issues of domestic and foreign policy (as subsequent sections of this study will demonstrate), the traditional evaluation of Grant as president nevertheless pays far less attention to them than to the corruption issue. Although their views have gained acceptance in the historical tradition, writers like Hesseltine and Nevins never have provided a full explanation of why the issue of corruption should eclipse the many other fundamental issues of Grant's presidency. As is the case with studies of President Grant's character, much of what has been passed down as an objective appraisal of the Grant administration more closely resembles the partisan critiques that were produced by a relatively small group of elite reformers during the 1870's. Although such a minority sometimes can be a source of enlightenment, in this case, it has contributed a monolithic picture of a complex era that is about as depressing as it is inaccurate. More recent historians have presented a similar picture, allowing casual verdicts on the "Sahara of malfeasance which was the Grant Administration."[45]

The foremost studies of the Grant presidency all offer surprisingly little insight into Grant's enemies and, if anything, tend simply to take the word of the reformers at face value. In *"The Best Men": Liberal Reformers in the Gilded Age*, John Sproat describes the unquestionable elitism of the reformers, who saw themselves as the "'best men'—the intellectuals, the men of substance and breeding . . . [They] seemed almost to be exiles in their own land, watching in impotent dismay as

---

[45] Armbruster, p. 206.

their countrymen gorged themselves at the 'great barbecue.'"[46]   This small but influential "collection of intellectuals, publicists, and professionals," Eric Foner points out, had, of course, styled *themselves* "best men."[47]   Historians have agreed with the self-appraisal of reformers, concurring as well that Grant and most of his political allies fall outside the category of "best men," or, to use terms that are found in Hesseltine, "thinking men," "men of property and intelligence."[48]

The backdrop of the drama of the sacrifice of reform to "Grantism" suggests an analysis that emphasizes literary impressions over the historical record. A more careful examination of the political situation during the 1870's calls the reformers' portrait into question. The period was marked by unusually bitter political conflict not only between Republicans and Democrats, but also within the dominant Republican Party. Hesseltine goes as far as to say that the "fierce political warfare supplanted and almost surpassed in bitterness the military conflict of the four preceding years."[49]   The war between Andrew Johnson and Radical Republicans in Congress hardly set the stage for a second "Era of Good Feelings," and although many thought that Grant's entry into the White House would establish a new harmony, the new president's opposition presented a series of contradictions that most histories of the period fail to analyze.

Faced with a Congress that had prevailed over the previous president and which cherished its role in executive appointments, Grant displayed his independence when he selected his cabinet without consulting party leaders, a step that caused widespread condemnation from Congress. Grant's first cabinet contained both Radicals who had followed traditional practices of appointment through the dominant patronage system, such as George S. Boutwell and John A.J. Creswell, and reformers who attempted to depart from such traditional practices with aspirations toward a merit-based system, such as Ebenezer R. Hoar and Jacob D. Cox.[50]   Grant seems to have seen himself as a president above parties and in favor of conciliation.[51]   While many criticized him as a political amateur, Hayes, who was substantially in the camp of the

---

[46]   Sproat, p. vii.
[47]   Foner, p. 488.
[48]   Hesseltine, pp. 319, 341, 364.
[49]   Ibid., p. vii.
[50]   Benedict, pp. 361-62; Hoogenboom, p. 53; Hoogenboom in Morgan, p. 79.
[51]   Young, *Around the World* II, pp. 359-60.

reformers, praised the cabinet: "It seems to mean business and not political scheming. It is an attempt to put fitness and qualifications before what is called 'claims' and 'political services.' If anybody could overthrow the spoils doctrine and practice, Grant is the man."[52]

It is important to realize that Grant began his presidency with a clear desire to remain above factionalism, but it is equally important to understand that the actions that gave rise to his first cabinet were the product of the president's inexperience in elective office.[53] Once in office, he discovered that the practical realities of politics made it preferable for the sake of insuring policy successes to depart, at least to some extent, from his initial reluctance to consult congressmen when making appointments. As Grant later observed, "An Executive must consider Congress. A government machine must run, and an Executive depends on Congress. The members have their rights as well as himself." Cooperation with Congress, he felt, was desirable to "have the government go smoothly, and secure wholesome legislation . . . ."[54]

Some historians have made the mistake of equating Grant's decision to accommodate the requests of certain congressmen with a surrender to the legislative branch, but Grant actually was taking steps that would prove instrumental in securing his many policy successes. Over the course of his administration, Grant's ongoing relationship with Radicals—a group of practical politicians who in the 1870's also would be branded as Stalwarts or spoilsmen—evoked outcries of corruption from reformers who felt excluded from power and position in government. Following this sentiment is a whole series of assertions permeating the traditional consensus that view Grant's alliances with practical politicians as evidence of the president's poor judgment. Grant, it would seem, had a tendency to be manipulated by those who knew which buttons to push to attain the simple-minded president's support. "What Grant needs," Charles Eliot Norton wrote George William Curtis, ". . . is independent, sympathetic, intelligent, and

---

[52] Williams III, p. 59.

[53] "I don't believe," Joseph G. Rosengarten confided to pioneer civil service reformer Thomas A. Jenckes in March 1869, "a personal administration, such as the present Cabinet seems to be,—with no wish other than the President's and no counsel or advice or policy of its own, can or ought to be successful." Hoogenboom, p. 54.

[54] Young, *Around the World* II, p. 265.

trustworthy counselors. . . . He is easily influenced by what one may call *second-class ideas* if skilfully put before him . . . ."[55]

The criticisms of Grant's alliances lacked more substance than often has been thought. For example, Boutwell, an able Secretary of the Treasury, was the most vilified administrator of Grant's early cabinet.[56] Henry Adams considered him the personification of the spoils system and believed his name "suggested only a somewhat lugubrious joke . . . ."[57] Actually, Boutwell, who was charged with administering the executive department second in size only to the Post Office Department,[58] was a pioneer in the advancement of personnel administration who both enacted stringent examinations between 1870 and 1872 and oversaw the first competitive examination in the United States civil service in 1870.[59] Boutwell still wished to make political appointments, but in view of his administrative record, it is still odd that intense enmity would have existed between him and the reformers.[60]

Looking at the exit of reformers like Hoar and Cox, who left Grant's cabinet and subsequently criticized the administration, Bailey, in the tradition of Henry Adams, asserts that the Grant administration "thus mocked Darwinism with the survival of the unfittest."[61] Hesseltine and Nevins share the view of the consensus that reformers in Grant's cabinet marked the high point of the administration while the perseverance of practical politicians in Grant's circle of advisors sank the government to new depths.[62] Similarly, Grant's political alliance with congressional Radicals such as Benjamin Butler, an ardent spoilsman, has been viewed as one "in pursuit of vulgar ends by vulgar means."[63] The elitism behind such observations is unquestionable. (The extent to which historians embrace these views is surprising:

---

[55] Coolidge, p. 393.

[56] Hoogenboom in Morgan, p. 83.

[57] Ibid.; Adams, p. 263.

[58] Hoogenboom in Morgan, p. 81.

[59] Ibid., pp. 83-84. See also Hoogenboom, p. 69 ("[H]istorians relying mainly on such partisan sources as the *Nation* have overlooked Boutwell's reform activities. What was actually—from the standpoint of personnel administration—an enlightened regime has been renowned as a blatant example of the spoils system.").

[60] Hoogenboom in Morgan, p. 84; Hoogenboom, p. 69.

[61] Bailey, *Presidential Greatness*, p. 217.

[62] Hesseltine, p. 374; Nevins, pp. 832-33.

[63] Hesseltine, p. 365. See also Hoar I, p. 386.

Nevins, in a singular application of literary impressions to a seemingly concrete observation, asserts that in 1876 the Grant administration virtually collapsed in the midst of substandard appointees and overall demoralization in executive departments. This conclusion, which shall be discussed further, entirely lacks a substantive basis.[64])

Ironically, many reformers and their leaders, such men as Curtis,[65] Norton,[66] and the Adams brothers,[67] had themselves desired office

---

[64] Nevins, p. 811.

[65] A staunch Republican, Curtis supported the Lincoln administration as an editor of *Harper's Weekly* and became a powerful player in the Republican Party in New York. He was defeated in a run for Congress in 1864, tried to influence the distribution of patronage during Lincoln's term, and was offered a diplomatic post in Egypt. He did not oppose the spoils system until it stopped working for him and his allies. Hoogenboom in Morgan, pp. 75-76. Both Curtis and his allies were ignored by President Johnson and by politicians in general. A few weeks after losing a campaign to become senator in 1866, he first embraced civil service reform publicly. Ibid., p. 76. In 1870, Curtis lost what he thought was a lock on the nomination for governor at the New York State Republican Convention, and he was later appointed to head Grant's Civil Service Commission. Ibid., pp. 76-77. After a vacancy for the position of the New York surveyor was filled without adhering to the civil service commission rules, Curtis, though suffering from a serious illness, published a letter in the *New York Tribune* protesting that the appointment had been made without his knowledge or consent. Ibid., p. 77. Each of what he perceived to be snubs had increased his zeal for reform. After resigning as the commission's chairman in 1873, Curtis, "[i]gnored by the administration and unable to realize his political ambitions," returned to his editorial work and aggressively criticized the Grant administration for its civil service practices. Ibid., pp. 76-78.

[66] Norton, who came from a prestigious academic family, had a long-term interest in literature and was both a co-editor of the *North American Review* and a founder of the *Nation*. He grew disenchanted with the state of affairs after the Civil War and is said to have been suspicious of democracy. Ibid., p. 74. Still, he enthusiastically supported Grant in 1868 and wrote to Curtis, "Grant grows daily in my respect & confidence," soon after the election. Assuming Grant would award positions to reformers, Norton added, "If you see a perfectly fit and easy opportunity, I should be glad to have you use it to suggest my name as that of a suitable person for the mission to Holland or Belgium." Ibid., p. 75. Curtis did write Fish on Norton's behalf, but no appointment was forthcoming. A few months later, Norton bitterly denounced Grant for surrendering to politicians through "disgraceful" appointments that violated the spirit of reform. Ibid., p. 75; Hoogenboom, p. 62.

under the patronage system for themselves or their friends, and they became reformers only after being rejected; basically, they were challenging the system that had rejected them and their kind![68] "Since these men were the most articulate group in the land," observes John A. Carpenter, "they helped to create the lasting impression that the civil service was more corrupt and evil during the Grant administration than at any other time in the nation's history."[69] (It should not be surprising, for example, to see Henry Adams overlook Boutwell's true record in view of his belief that the secretary meant "total extinction for any one resembling Henry Adams."[70]) Hoogenboom offers an explanation for the ongoing historiographical success of the reformers:

> The typical historian has been too loose in applying the term "corruption." Specifically, he labels a politically partisan civil service corrupt rather than inefficient; he equates the spoils system with corruption when honest spoilsmen far outnumber dishonest ones; he pronounces Gilded Age politicians guilty of corruption for associating with corruptionists even while attacking guilt by association in his own day.

---

[67] In the spring of 1869, Henry Adams wrote, "My hopes of the new Administration have all been disappointed; it is far inferior to the last. My friends have almost all lost ground instead of gaining it as I hoped. My family is buried politically beyond recovery for years. I am becoming more and more isolated so far as allies go. I even doubt whether I can find an independent organ to publish my articles, so strong is the current against us." Hoogenboom, pp. 62-63. Adams could gain office neither for himself nor for his brother Charles Francis, Jr., treasurer of the pro-reform Social Science Association, to whom he wrote, "I can't get you an office. The only members of this Government that I have met are mere acquaintants, not friends, and I fancy no request of mine would be likely to call out a gush of sympathy." Ibid., p. 63. Hoogenboom somewhat sardonically observes, "The administration was presumptuous enough to ignore the Adams family." Later that year, Henry wrote that he and his brothers, Charles Francis, Jr., and John Quincy, were "up to the ears in politics and public affairs, and in time," he hoped, "we shall perhaps make our little mark." Ibid., p. 63.

[68] Carpenter, p. 116; Hoogenboom in Morgan, pp. 74-79. "[R]eformers recognized the evils of the spoils system only after it thwarted their ambitions." Hoogenboom in Morgan, p. 74.

[69] Carpenter, p. 116.

[70] Adams, p. 263. Adams customarily referred to himself in the third person in his autobiography.

One apparent reason why the historian has exaggerated the corruption of the Gilded Age is his desire to enliven lectures and writings. All the world loves a scandal, and the historian is loathe to abandon the pleasure of dispensing "vicarious sin." More basically, the historian dislikes the dominant forces in the Gilded Age.[71]

Benedict further pursues a criticism of reformers and calls into question a historical problem neglected by the traditional consensus: the failure to provide a clear definition of corruption. This may seem an obvious matter, but in fact it is not:

> [M]uch of what scholars have called corruption was merely the dominant mode of choosing government officials through the patronage system. Scholars have tended to accept the judgment of the anti-Grant reformers that this system was inherently corrupt, but that is a very questionable conclusion, and reformers had ulterior, political motives for making the charge.[72]

Grant himself perceived the flaw in the reformers' attacks. In his last annual message, he made it a point to apologize for any errors that were made under the patronage system, but he simultaneously pointed out "differences of opinion between the Executive . . . and writers and debaters . . . . It is not necessarily evidence of blunder on the part of the Executive because there are these differences of views."[73]

That two major political factions did not share so basic a view as the definition of corruption illustrates the magnitude of these "differences of views" and a peculiar dilemma for historians who have (consciously or unconsciously) accepted the views of reformers who were not a part of the government. Shortly after his presidency, Grant noted not only the questionable nature of the reformers' charges, but also the irrationality and inherent contradictions that stood behind their words and their actions:

> Men will do things who are senators or members that reformers call corrupt. They will ask for patronage, and govern themselves in their dealings with the administration by their success in the matter of patronage. This is a custom, and if the reformer's theory is correct, it is

---

[71] Hoogenboom in Morgan, p. 71.
[72] Benedict, p. 376.
[73] Richardson IX, pp. 4353-54.

corruption. And yet the men who were reformers, who turned their eyes at the sins of others, I generally found as anxious for patronage as others. . . . In a government where there are senators and members, where senators and members depend upon politics for success, there will be applications for patronage. You cannot call it corruption—it is a condition of our representative form of government—and yet if you read the newspapers, and hear the stories of the reformers, you will be told that any asking for place is corruption . . . . There is a good deal of cant about civil service reform, which throws doubt upon the sincerity of the movement. The impression is given by the advocates of civil service reform that most of the executive appointments are made out of the penitentiary. Writers who have reached years of discretion, like John Jay [grandson of the founding father], gravely assert that one-fourth of the revenue collected at the New York Custom House is lost in the process of collection. Of course, no reform can be sound when it is sustained by such wild and astounding declarations. Then many of those who talk civil service reform in public are the most persistent in seeking offices for their friends. . . . [T]here is an immense amount of human nature in members of Congress, and it is in human nature to seek power and use it and to help friends. . . . It has become the habit of Congressmen to share with the Executive in the responsibility of appointments. It is unjust to say that this habit is necessarily corrupt. It is simply a custom that has grown up, a fact that cannot be ignored.[74]

The New York Customhouse to which Grant referred was the best known and most maligned office in government service, but as historians usually fail to realize, its administration actually improved during the Grant administration. In January 1866, fraud, waste, and incompetence were rampant, and removal rates ran very high for the next five years, but these trends would be replaced by a marked improvement after Grant appointed an adept administrator named Chester A. Arthur as the collector of the Customhouse in 1871.[75]

---

[74] Young, *Around the World* II, pp. 263-65.

[75] Hoogenboom in Morgan, p. 84. An 1874 law abolishing the moiety system and reducing the incomes of collectors contributed to the reform of the office. During the Hayes administration, the collectorship of the New York Customhouse became a showcase for reform after a long and highly publicized struggle in which Hayes ultimately succeeded in removing Arthur and naval officer Alonzo Cornell. Although the subsequent administration of the Customhouse continued to improve under Arthur's successor, and although historians have followed the trend of making the situation a showcase for the triumph of reform over the spoils system under Grant, Hayes' actions were

President Johnson's Revenue Commission estimated in January 1866 that the New York Customhouse lost $12 to $25 million annually. The Grant Civil Service Commission under Curtis' leadership applied the earlier figures in 1872 and estimated that one-fourth of the annual federal revenue was lost in collection. Liberal Republican Senator Lyman Trumbull, citing the commission's report, charged the supposedly corrupt Grant regime with losing $95,830,986.22 of the national revenue.[76] When a Grant supporter demanded a justification for this charge, the commission responded that its estimate was intended to provide the "most forceable illustration of the mischief of the system" and actually dated from "the administration of Andrew Johnson when the evils of the 'spoils' system culminated."[77] The loss recorded referred to money owed to the government and never collected, not money collected and then stolen; the deficiencies and misappropriations under the internal revenue law had dropped to one-seventh of those suffered during the Johnson administration. "We regret," the commissioners stated, "that in our desire to divest our report of any partisan character whatever and to make it as concise as possible, we failed to explain this statement, more in detail, & to show how ingenious and successful were the efforts of the administration to prevent the loss to which we alluded." Interested in painting as bleak a picture as possible to demonstrate the need for reform, the commission knowingly had used obsolete figures since it was aware of the improvement that had taken place under Grant. "The commission could hardly afford to have the spoils system reformed by spoilsmen,"[78] Hoogenboom notes.

The matter of whether patronage is synonymous with corruption—a fundamental premise of the reformers' charges and the traditional consensus—provides a serious question not only of accuracy, but of consistency; for historians, if the reformers' verdict is true, must explain how Grant's predecessors, most of whom practiced patronage (especially since Jackson),[79] led administrations that evade the brand of

---

intended not as reform, but as the displacement of the Stalwart Republican Roscoe Conkling machine with remnants of the old "reform" Republican Reuben Fenton machine. Ibid., p. 87.

[76] Ibid., p. 72.

[77] Ibid., pp. 72-73.

[78] Ibid., p. 73.

[79] See Hoogenboom, pp. 5-7.

large-scale corruption that marks Grant's presidency. Lincoln himself boasted that his administration had "distributed to it's party friends as nearly all the civil patronage as any administration ever did"[80] and gave his enthusiastic support to several of Grant's future allies, including quintessential spoilsmen Roscoe Conkling and Zachariah Chandler.[81] Lincoln utilized the support of politicos to help secure his renomination, caring less about their support of administration bills than about the former goal.[82] Grant, whose use of the patronage system was certainly no greater than that of his two immediate predecessors, expected support for administration measures from his congressional allies as well as help in securing his renomination. In assessing the causes of such inconsistencies, greater attention should be given the changing predispositions of historians when their analysis shifts from one presidency to another.

What is ironic about the traditional picture of honest reformers opposing the president's corrupt party henchmen is the fact that Grant was the first president since the establishment of the Jacksonian spoils system to initiate civil service reform. In his Second Annual Message in 1870, Grant issued an earnest call for civil service reform, and his efforts were instrumental in establishing the nation's first civil service commission.[83] Grant appointed Curtis, the leader of the civil service reform movement, as the commission's chairman, and the president proceeded to oust 192 government officials who had been shown to be corrupt or inefficient.[84] The commission, which made use of competitive examinations, was the precursor of the modern civil service system that followed the Pendleton Act of 1883. By 1875, after Congress refused to appropriate funds to continue the commission, Grant seems to have regarded the experiment in reform as one of "questionable utility" and later would recall that "[o]ne of the most brilliant candidates before the civil service board was in jail very soon

---

[80] Donald, p. 76. Under Lincoln's administration, "1,457 incumbents of the 1,639 presidential offices were removed. In addition, the occupants of many offices were changed two and three times between 1861 and 1865." Hoogenboom, p. 6.

[81] Donald, p. 77; George, pp. 97, 200.

[82] Donald, p. 77.

[83] Richardson IX, p. 4063; Hesseltine, p. 252.

[84] Hesseltine, pp. 253, 264; White, p. 282.

after his appointment, for robbery."[85] Grant disbanded the commission in 1875, though the president's power to set rules governing the civil service remained intact, and civil service reform as defined by the reformers entered a stalemate that was not broken until the Pendleton Act.[86]

The issue of a workable merit system in the American constitutional system is itself a problematic one that deserves reconsideration from both historians and political scientists: the further detachment of an expanding bureaucracy from the influence of elected officials, a practical result of the system advocated by Gilded Age reformers and their successors, the Progressives, has prompted observations about inefficiency and corruption that seem as bleak as the picture painted by the reformers. The extent of the subsequent improvement in the modern bureaucracy remains a matter of serious debate. In the face of bureaucratic failure, the long-accepted idea of the Progressive model as an ideal form of public administration has become increasingly subject to attack in recent years.

Returning, however, to the issue of Grant's enemies and the commission that was in effect between 1871 and 1875, there can be little question that by the standards of the reformers, the commission was a major step in the direction of civil service reform.[87] Leonard D. White's *The Republican Era: 1869-1901* views the establishment of a merit system as one of the crowning achievements of the period between Grant and William McKinley.[88] Although the process was a gradual one, the civil service commission established under Grant was second only to the Pendleton Act in decisiveness as a step toward establishing a merit system as defined by the reformers. The 1883 act, furthermore, came only after a traumatic event shook the nation. Civil service reform during Grant's term was not supported by rising industrialists, urban laborers, or rural farmers. Only after Garfield's assassination by an insane office seeker in 1881 did there arise a decisive popular advocacy for the prescription of civil service reformers.[89] Uncompromising reformers in the 1870's did not serve

---

[85] Young, *Around the World* II, p. 268.

[86] White, pp. 283-84.

[87] See Hoogenboom, pp. 91, 95, 126.

[88] White, pp. 379, 394.

[89] Hoogenboom in Morgan, p. 90.

their purported cause very well by attacking a president who displayed unprecedented sympathy on an issue of concern to a clear minority.

Although he sometimes would make exceptions to the rules of the commission, the record clearly reflects the president's dedication to the effort until deciding in 1874 that he was open to disbanding the commission. That decision came only after Grant acknowledged that he was substantially alone in the reform, adding a statement reflective of his seemingly irrational inability to receive non-condemnatory appraisals from reformers: "Generally the support which this reform receives is from those who give it their support only to find fault when the rules are apparently departed from."[90]

Those historians who presuppose the legitimacy of the reform movement's attacks on Grant based upon corruption and its subsequent formation of the Liberal Republican Party to oppose the president have failed to consider a very basic fact about the situation as the presidential election year of 1872 was approaching. As the Liberal Republicans were forming their movement, not a single major scandal had been uncovered in high office since Grant's inauguration, and the civil service commission was firmly intact. Discomfort with the "corruption" of the Grant administration could be based on little more than Grant's alliance with many practical politicians and the reformers' questionable definition of corruption. When viewed in the context of the actual events of the time, the dissatisfaction of the reformers calls into question the legitimacy of their charges from the standpoint of historians. As Sproat points out:

> Liberal Republicanism essentially was a movement to rid the Republican party of Grantism . . . . But it was far from a pure reform effort, for many Liberal Republicans were interested chiefly in promoting their personal fortunes at the expense of Grant and his followers. . . . Grant's failure as President was a "pitiful story, one of the most pitiful in political history," as [Edwin L.] Godkin observed; but there was no universal agreement among the delegates who gathered at Cincinnati in 1872 as to exactly where and how the President had failed. They all conceded only that he should be defeated in the coming election.[91]

---

[90] Richardson IX, p. 4255.

[91] Sproat, p. 76.

Ironically, the reformers' condemnatory portrait of Gilded Age politics as a series of selfish attempts to gain office by unprincipled politicos—a portrait that the traditional consensus tends to accept— remarkably resembles their own primary motives and the questionable, often reckless charges of corruption that were casually made in order to fulfill those motives. This is not to say that the reformers did not oppose Grant on substantive policy matters; it remains to be shown that one area of policy makes a critical difference in understanding both Grant and the reformers. However, as far as matters of corruption or substandard appointments are concerned, the reformers' actual grievance seems to be that the president was not distributing enough patronage to reformers; in view of the fact that none of Grant's major appointees proved either corrupt or inefficient as of 1872, there seems no logical alternative to this explanation.

As Hoogenboom observes, "the civil service reform movement fits into a pattern of those out of power versus those in power. Reformers invariably wished to curtail the appointing power after they thought it had been abused, and to them abuse occurred when men of their own social station or political faction were not appointed to office."[92] Behind the reformers' demands there seems to be a sense of desperation for power and consequently a failure to take into account the practical realities of the situation. As Coolidge points out, a reform that was advocated by a relatively small group of elites that would transform methods of politics was a lower priority than issues "involving the perpetuity of government itself"—"the maintenance of our prestige abroad, the safeguarding of American lives and property on foreign soil, the rigid execution of the law at home, [and] the firm establishment of public credit."[93]

While Grant is criticized widely by the traditional consensus as a man without experience or knowledge of civil affairs, it is ironically his critics—the group whose views have been endorsed by the consensus— who usually were more inexperienced and detached from the practical demands of high office while Grant was president. Grant could have striven to become more like John Quincy Adams, a hero of the reformers and the last president before him to take a significant step toward civil service reform. It should be remembered, however, that Adams' efforts to install an elite meritocracy were part of a general

---

[92] Hoogenboom in Morgan, p. 79.
[93] Coolidge, pp. 401-03.

outlook on governance that ignored the practical realities of American politics and led to an administration that consequently met with little success either in matters of policy or in gaining popular acceptance.[94] One wonders whether Grant would have done more for his reputation in history books had he traveled down the same path.

Although most of what historians have branded as corruption rests on highly debatable grounds, there were clear cases of corruption that deserve analysis. When taking corruption into account in an overall appraisal of Grant as president, four considerations should be kept in mind:

I. Any direct responsibility for corruption on the part of Grant himself, or any deliberate attempt to obstruct the prosecution of a corrupt subordinate (i.e., cover-up), would justify the most serious indictment of the president.

II. If Grant displayed serious character or leadership flaws that allowed corruption to run rampant on high levels, despite any direct involvement on his part, and if he displayed apathy toward purging it, a lesser indictment may be in order.

III. If charges of corruption were raised for which Grant bore no responsibility, direct or indirect, but the president's accusers nevertheless were able to weaken the administration—and thus its capacity for achievement—the resulting appraisal may be less laudatory to the extent that potential achievements were diminished.

IV. Whatever standards are applied in assessing the impact of the corruption issue on a general appraisal of Grant as president should remain consistent with standards that are applied to other presidencies.

I.

However condemnatory the traditional consensus has been, Grant's personal honesty has never been questioned by serious scholars.[95] It is also agreed that the president never benefited personally from

---

[94] Ketcham, pp. 138-40, 157.

[95] In part for reasons to be explained, this study does not hold McFeely's novel charge that Grant perjured himself in 1876 to protect a subordinate (accompanying footnote 142) to be supported by any sober application of available evidence.

corruption. Those who charge that Grant defended corrupt subordinates simultaneously infer that it was the president's naïveté, a genuine belief in their innocence, that accounts for his actions. Thus the first consideration is not an issue for Grant.

II.

The traditional consensus casts its verdict based upon the second consideration. However, even charges of what might consensually be termed the "real" corruption of the Grant administration (as opposed to the more haphazard definition of corruption that was used by the reformers) are more groundless than the traditional consensus would have one believe. In order to understand this assessment, historians should consider that charges of "real" corruption under Grant fall under one of four categories: 1. cases of actual corruption for which Grant bore no responsibility, either directly or indirectly; 2. events that took place while Grant was president that historians construe to be "scandals," but which refer merely to disturbing developments for which Grant was clearly not accountable; 3. irresponsible charges of corruption against Grant's subordinates; and 4. well-founded charges of corruption on high levels of the Grant administration. While the ingredients of a solid indictment of President Grant on the grounds that he allowed corruption to run rampant would rely on those events that belong to the fourth category, the vast majority of what are commonly termed the Grant scandals actually belong to the other three categories.

1. Looking at the first category, the Credit Mobilier, the most conspicuous of the so-called Grant scandals, was only uncovered during the Grant administration in 1872. The corrupt activity, which involved the bribery of several congressmen and did not directly concern the executive branch, had occurred in 1867-68, before Grant even became president, yet no scandal has become as synonymous with "Grantism" as the Credit Mobilier.[96] Nowhere else in the American historical tradition is a president held accountable for a major scandal that took place before he assumed office, and as Bailey effectively observes, "We could as fairly blame President Benjamin Harrison for the Johnstown flood of 1889."[97] Equally surprising is the frequent (though not

---

[96] Hesseltine, pp. 309-10.
[97] Bailey, *Presidential Greatness*, p. 109.

universal) inclusion of the Tweed Ring, a strictly municipal scandal that involved the misdeeds of William Marcy ("Boss") Tweed, a New York City Democrat, in accounts of the corruption of the Grant administration. The Tweed Ring was formed during Johnson's presidency and was only uncovered during Grant's term, but these facts are irrelevant since neither president was remotely connected to it.[98]

Second to the Credit Mobilier in magnitude as a scandal of the Grant era—accepting, of course, the traditional consensus' definition of the Grant scandals—was the Whiskey Ring, which involved networks of whiskey distillers who had been defrauding the government for years. Like the Tweed Ring, the Whiskey Ring was born during Johnson's term, and it was only uncovered while Grant was in the White House.[99] Although one might use the fact that the ring, which after all was connected to the executive branch, continued to thrive through a portion of the Grant era as a justification for labelling it a Grant scandal, it would be absurd to attribute the Whiskey Ring to any deficiencies on Grant's part; the same might be said of Johnson, assessments of whom rightfully are not affected by the scandal. The ring's members clearly occupied levels of government that were too low to implicate reasonably either president for negligence, and Grant actually would play an impressive role in the prosecution of the culprits. The only problematic feature of the Whiskey Ring for Grant would be the events that followed the questionable allegations that were levelled against his private secretary, Orville Babcock, a situation that will merit further analysis as a component of the third category of scandal.

2. Turning to the second category, most traditional accounts of the Grant presidency discuss events under the heading of "scandal" which might be disturbing, but which do not even involve questions about corruption that should have a negative bearing on assessments of Grant. One example is the "Salary Grab," a bill that, while including several necessary pay raises, also gave congressmen a virtual $5,000 retroactive bonus. The act, which later was modified after being met by widespread public opposition, was a troubling example of the greed of Congress, but it was not illegal and holds little relevance in appraisals of Grant's record as president.[100]

---

[98] Ibid.
[99] Hesseltine, p. 378.
[100] Hoogenboom, p. 70; Nevins, p. 612.

A more consistently misrepresented "scandal" is the attempt by Jay Gould and James Fisk to corner the gold market on "Black Friday," September 24, 1869, an event which more accurately should be termed a near-calamity than a scandal. Gould and Fisk had conspired with Grant's brother-in-law, Abel R. Corbin, to influence the president's policy on the monthly sale of government gold in order to insure the success of their plan. Although Grant actually foiled the scheme, the facts of this case usually are distorted to infer that it marked a major blunder on the part of the president, who Nevins asserts erred "by showing that he was the willing associate of men notorious for financial trickery and legalized robbery . . . and by demonstrating that he and Secretary Boutwell failed to see through a fairly transparent conspiracy against the nation's economic stability, and dealt with it irresolutely and tardily."[101]

Neither charge is justified by the facts. Corbin did manipulate his brother-in-law's visits to him to bring him into the company of Gould and Fisk, especially the former, but the president met their attempts to influence him not to sell government gold with coldness and distrust, expressing privately his suspicion of their motives. Grant also rebuked Corbin for admitting Gould to his house.[102] Far from failing to detect that a dangerous financial scheme was under way, Grant sent a vigilant letter to Boutwell on September 12:

> I am satisfied that . . . you will be met by the bulls and bears of Wall street, and probably by merchants too, to induce you to sell gold, or pay the November interest in advance, on the one side, and to hold fast on the other. The fact is, a desperate struggle is now taking place, and each party want[s] the government to help them out. I write this letter to advise you of what I think you may expect, to put you on your guard.[103]

Operating under the mistaken assumption that Corbin had persuaded Grant, Gould and Fisk created a panic on "Black Friday" when they attempted to corner the gold market, but their plans were upset when Grant ordered the sale of $4 million in government gold, which ended

---

[101] Nevins, pp. 282-83.

[102] Hesseltine, pp. 171-77; Nevins, p. 284.

[103] Grant, *Papers* XIX, pp. 243-44. See also Boutwell, *Reminiscences* II, pp. 169-70.

the panic.[104]   That such basic evidence as Grant's letter to Boutwell is usually overlooked while the entire episode is construed as an example of the president's naiveté, ignoring the acuteness he displayed during the crisis, is yet another example of the substandard analysis that mars the traditional verdict of the Grant presidency.

3. Proceeding to the third category of scandal during Grant's presidency, a reconsideration of the charges that were made against the president's high-level appointees calls into question the judgment of the traditional consensus that Grant was naively loyal to corrupt subordinates. Interestingly enough, there is a major discrepancy among different studies both in mentioning and in appraising the validity of charges that were made concerning the alleged corruption of various cabinet members.   Grant made a total of 25 cabinet appointments during his presidency—a record he shares with Franklin D. Roosevelt,[105] whose term was over four years longer—and of this number, only one has left historians a solid case of corruption: Secretary of War William W. Belknap.[106]   Additionally, Secretary of State Fish, Attorney General Amos T. Akerman, and Postmaster General Creswell have been ranked among the most capable people ever to hold their respective positions in American history.[107]   Nevins asserts that except for Fish, Grant "had systematically gotten rid of the ablest and most upright of his Cabinet officers within a short time after their appointment," but this judgment relies upon the author's embrace of the supposed "men of cultivation, urbane knowledge of the world, and interest in reform" to the exclusion of the "political swine" who were the spoilsmen.[108]

Actually, of those cabinet members who served long enough to leave   appraisable   records—notwithstanding   the   numerous unsubstantiated attacks made by partisan opponents and the traditional consensus on those who were spoilsmen—none left records of overall inefficiency, though Secretary of the Treasury William A. Richardson was duped in a case that could fairly be construed as indicating his negligence.   Nevertheless, several studies leave the reader with the

---

[104] Hesseltine, pp. 171-79.
[105] Taylor, p. 218.
[106] Nevins, pp. 832-33.
[107] See "The Ten Best Secretaries of State—and the Five Worst," p. 78; Barnhart, p. 4; Nevins, p. 139.
[108] Nevins, pp. 832-33, 137.

impression fostered by Woodward that all but a few cabinet members were "nonentities and crooks" and that "[c]orruption spread like an epidemic through the Cabinet . . . ."[109] An example of irresponsible history-writing, "The Lowest Ebb," Woodward's 1957 *American Heritage* article about Grant's presidency, goes as far as to charge Attorney General George H. Williams, Richardson, and Secretary of the Interior Columbus Delano with corruption in order to support this view.[110]

Williams, Richardson, Delano, and a fourth cabinet member— Secretary of the Navy George M. Robeson—were all the targets of unjustified charges of corruption, and all four cases are recounted differently by different narratives, a reflection of the lack of consistency that one finds behind the historiography of the Grant presidency. Most accounts fail even to mention one or more of these cases, and a look at the two most definitive studies, Hesseltine's and Nevins', reveals a further tendency to devote more attention to such issues when they contribute to a more condemnatory portrait of the Grant administration. Nevins devotes considerable space to the details of the charges against all four men and maximizes the doubt of his readers as to their innocence by citing approvingly several contemporaries who backed those charges.[111] Hesseltine's more sober analysis of these issues does not infer that any of these men were guilty of corruption, but the author also devotes substantially less space to them than Nevins; in fact, Hesseltine evidently does not see the charges against Robeson as being worthy of mention.[112]

In 1873, Grant nominated Attorney General Williams to be chief justice, and while the Senate Judiciary Committee was considering the nominee, it was discovered that Williams' wife had purchased an expensive carriage and liveries for two servants from the Justice Department's contingent fund. Additionally, it was learned, Williams kept his accounts on government payrolls. The charges, though true, were quite minor—they involved indiscretions rather than outright corruption or illegality on Williams' part—but the attorney general was already unpopular in political circles, and he subsequently fell under fire for corruption without having committed acts to justify the

---

[109] C.V. Woodward, pp. 56, 107.
[110] Ibid., p. 107.
[111] Nevins, pp. 714, 764-65, 769-75, 789, 816.
[112] Hesseltine, pp. 362-64, 374, 376-77.

charge.[113]   Sometimes known as Grant's "Secretary of State for Southern affairs," Williams had a strong record as attorney general, and it was with reluctance that the president, who perceived that the recklessness of the attack on Williams did not fit any indiscretions as much as the opposition of his political enemies, eventually withdrew his name as a nominee for chief justice.[114]

Richardson fell under fire for corruption after it was discovered in 1874 that John D. Sanborn, with whom the treasury secretary had made contracts to seek out delinquent taxes, proceeded to pocket a moiety of 50% of the $427,000 that was collected, an action that, though not blatantly illegal in itself, included fraudulent transactions.[115]   Those who were closely connected to the case, including members of the House committee that investigated the Sanborn contracts, realized that Richardson was innocent of any corruption in the matter, though he could be charged with negligence.[116]   Grant realized this as well and hoped to avert the political damage that might come from those who would be quick to use an imminent House resolution censuring Richardson as further fuel for framing him in the matter. He reached an understanding with the House that Richardson would resign and gave him a lesser appointment on the Court of Claims.[117]   In the final analysis, Hoogenboom finds the incident most important in illustrating that the collection of moieties, which contrary to common impression had ancient roots and was not a new invention, was actually eliminated in 1874 due to the public's adverse reaction to the Sanborn contracts; their resentment fostered improving administrative efficiency during the Gilded Age.[118]

In 1875, Delano was charged with involvement in corrupt land transactions in Wyoming, but the charges were unfounded. Grant both defended the secretary and refused to accept his resignation while the public accusations persisted, feeling that resignation would "be accepted as an admission of the charges."[119]

---

[113] Ibid., pp. 361-62; White, p. 369.
[114] Hesseltine, p. 374.
[115] Coolidge, pp. 439-40; Hesseltine, pp. 363-64.
[116] Hoar I, p. 328; Coolidge, pp. 440-41.
[117] Coolidge, pp. 440-41.
[118] Hoogenboom in Morgan, p. 70.
[119] Hesseltine, pp. 376-77; Nevins, p. 775.

The next year, the Democratic House of Representatives conducted a series of penetrating investigations for the purpose of embarrassing Grant that exceeded in ferocity the previous attacks of Liberal Republicans. Even Hesseltine admits that these investigations were transparent and generally unsuccessful attempts to humiliate the president, and the fact that Grant handled them with finesse was not enough to stop the House.[120]

Among these clearly partisan efforts was an investigation that aimed for the impeachment of Robeson, who was probed principally because he had become rich during his term. Investigations of the navy secretary's connection to A.G. Cattell and Company, the firm that had made him rich, uncovered no direct evidence of corruption, and little came of the House's simultaneous attempt to tie the extravagant operation of navy yards to Robeson's inefficiency.[121] The House failed to follow a July 1876 request by the investigating committee to pursue the impeachment of Robeson, and the clear lack of evidence of the secretary's corruption, combined with the fact that charges of Navy Department extravagance did not even constitute any "high crimes and misdemeanors" (the prerequisites for impeachment), reflects the questionable nature of the investigation.[122] (Actually, Garfield pointed out that the investigating committee had not come up with one valid charge of illegality.[123]) Robeson remained in Grant's cabinet until the end of his term.

The cases of Williams, Richardson, Delano, and Robeson are relatively minor issues in the history of the Grant administration, even from the standpoint of the traditional consensus. While loyalty to subordinates under fire, provided that he was convinced of their innocence, was certainly one of Grant's character traits, from these cases there appears to be little basis for the contention that this loyalty fostered corruption in government. Although the record shows Grant's subordinates virtually to have been framed by unfounded charges of corruption, most historians evidently see this seemingly minor point as

---

[120] Hesseltine, pp. 378-94.

[121] Nevins, pp. 815-16; White, pp. 369-70; Coolidge, pp. 160-61. While Nevins and White write with criticism of Robeson, Coolidge describes the secretary as "a man of brilliant qualities" whose criticisms were undeserved. Coolidge, p. 389.

[122] Nevins, p. 816; Coolidge, p. 160; White, p. 370.

[123] Garfield III, p. 328.

negligible, and many perpetuate the charges of Grant's more reckless enemies.

The broader meaning of unjustified charges of corruption by Grant's enemies, whether one looks at these cases or at the reformers' tendency to equate the practice of the spoils system with corruption, has consistently eluded historians. Each charge of corruption, founded or unfounded, should not be viewed merely as isolated incidents. In order to present a coherent understanding of the Grant presidency, they should be viewed together as part of a broader picture. An understanding of the recklessness of the charges made by Grant's enemies is necessary when assessing the president's defense of Orville Babcock during the more complex case of the Whiskey Ring.

It was Secretary of the Treasury Benjamin H. Bristow who uncovered the Whiskey Ring in 1875, and historians tend to forget the positive role that Grant played in backing the prosecution of the culprits who were involved. The over 350 Whiskey Ring indictments that resulted from Bristow's efforts are eclipsed in traditional studies by Grant's defense of Babcock in 1876, widely viewed as a symptom of "the President's pitiful inability to suspect any of his appointees of any wrong," in the words of Maxim Armbruster.[124] This rash assessment clearly overlooks the facts. During the ring's investigation, Grant had received a letter suggesting that Babcock might be among the guilty, and he responded to this suggestion by forwarding the letter to Bristow along with an unequivocal endorsement of a stringent prosecution:

> . . . I forward this for information and to the end that if it throws any light upon new parties to summon as witnesses they may be brought out. *Let no guilty man escape if it can be avoided.* Be especially vigilant—or instruct those engaged in the prosecution of fraud to be—against all who insinuate that they have high influence to protect—or to protect them. No personal consideration should stand in the way of performing a public duty.[125]

Bristow made certain to publish this endorsement despite the fact that it was marked "confidential," and Nevins observes that "there is some ground for believing that he issued it without permission . . . ."[126]

---

[124] Hesseltine, p. 384; Armbruster, p. 204.
[125] Nevins, p. 788.
[126] Ibid.

Far from displaying an inability (or a refusal) to suspect a subordinate of wrongdoing, Grant made efforts to learn of any evidence there was against Babcock and told Attorney General Edwards Pierrepont, who was assisting Bristow with the prosecutions, that "if Babcock is guilty, there is no man who wants him so proven guilty as I do, for it is the greatest piece of traitorism to me that a man could possibly practice."[127] As Bristow and Pierrepont worked to investigate him, Babcock protested his innocence, publicly demanding a trial,[128] and the evidence against him was dubious.[129] Pierrepont, one of the best lawyers of his time, whose recorded comments indicate that he was sincere in the desire to pursue Babcock, simultaneously cautioned that the evidence against him should justify indictment, lest the administration be embarrassed; Bristow did not share this concern.[130] Furthermore, many observers alleged that Babcock's indictment, which came in December 1875, was intended to discredit the administration, a view that Grant came to share, and while this might seem a naive conclusion, there are strong grounds to reconsider whether Bristow's prosecution of Babcock was legitimate.[131]

Historians usually view Grant's famous "Let no guilty man escape" message with contempt as they point to his seemingly hypocritical opposition to Bristow's prosecution of Babcock, but the traditional consensus makes the mistake of accepting Bristow on his own terms without reserve. Grant's position during Bristow's prosecution of Babcock cannot be fully appreciated without understanding the usually underemphasized context in which the Secretary of the Treasury was operating. Bristow's concurrence with Grant on economic matters had set the stage for his adept management of the Treasury Department after he was appointed in 1874, but the secretary was also a zealous reformer who found himself at odds with the practical politicians who were

---

[127] Hesseltine, pp. 384-86.

[128] Ibid., p. 385.

[129] The principal piece of evidence in question was a cryptic letter signed "Sylph" from Babcock to General John A. McDonald, a close associate and the supervisor of internal revenue who headed the Whiskey Ring, that read as follows: "I have succeeded. They will not go. I will write you." Nevins, pp. 762, 788. Babcock denied the letter had any connection with the Ring. Ibid., p. 789.

[130] Hesseltine, p. 409; Webb, p. 198; Nevins, p. 791.

[131] Hesseltine, pp. 385-86; Nevins, pp. 791-92, 788; Webb, p. 198.

serving under the president. The appeal of his impressive performance as secretary to conservative financial interests, combined with his spreading fame as a reformer, made him a contender for the presidency, and it is clear that he became ambitious to enter the White House.[132]

While historians have never even acknowledged the possibility that Bristow was a man who would use corrupt means to achieve his aspirations, he did have a recognizable tendency to apply his reformative zeal toward attacks on those who seemed to stand in the way of his ambitions. By December 1874, before he even had much knowledge of the Whiskey Ring, Bristow had concluded that there was a conspiracy led by Delano and Babcock to persuade Grant to oust him from the cabinet. He proceeded to talk at length with Fish and various congressmen who visited his department about his suspicions of Delano's intrigue, and he undoubtedly contributed to the interior secretary's declining reputation within Washington circles as charges were levelled against him during the spring of 1875.[133]   The conflict between Delano and Bristow led each man to attack the other publicly during the summer, and it was Delano rather than Bristow who was the first to exit the cabinet.[134]

With Delano gone, Bristow had to contend with only two major obstacles: Babcock and "the third term menace"—the reformers' fear that Grant would seek a third term in 1876 and consequently keep his henchmen in control of the Republican Party to the exclusion of the party's "better" elements.[135]   Even if Bristow's effort to undermine Delano were not unprovoked or distorted by his presidential ambitions, there is little justification for a cabinet member perpetuating alarm over the possibility that the president might seek reelection, regardless of whether the third-term rumors were true (and they were not). In March 1875, Bristow expressed to Garfield, an Ohio congressman at the time, his regret that Grant was "really meditating a third term" and drew "a sombre picture" of how undesirable men had taken over the White House with the intention of keeping Grant in power.[136]   Garfield proceeded to write his Ohio friends on Bristow's behalf, advising them that "we must throw off the third-term nightmare before we can have

---

[132] Hesseltine, pp. 376, 395; Nevins, p. 764.
[133] Nevins, pp. 763, 765; Hesseltine, p. 376.
[134] Nevins, p. 776; Hesseltine, pp. 376-77.
[135] Hesseltine, p. 376.
[136] Garfield III, p. 39; Hesseltine, p. 377.

any party success. . . . We must in plain and unmistakable words for ourselves repudiate the doctrine of a third term."[137]

Nevins' observation that Bristow was "perfectly loyal to Grant" does not quite convey the entire situation.[138] While Grant had made honest efforts to explore the charges against Babcock, the only major impediment to face Bristow since the president openly repudiated any desire for a third term in May 1875, Grant eventually concluded that Babcock's prosecution was a product of suspect motives.[139] In Saint Louis, where Babcock was indicted "for conspiracy to defraud the revenue," many spoke of a "rebel grand jury" that "was trying to indict the whole Administration," an impression that spread through much of Washington. Treasury Department agents working on the whiskey cases shared the view that Bristow would become president as a result of the investigations. Pierrepont himself became convinced that Babcock's indictment was irresponsible and that it aimed merely to discredit the administration.[140]

Thus Grant had ample reason to suspect Bristow's motives, and his decision to make a deposition defending Babcock, which was delivered before the chief justice on February 17, 1876, cannot be explained merely by the traditional consensus' platitudes about the president's gullibility. Historians frequently have displayed a naiveté in analyzing Bristow's prosecution that ironically resembles the same trait that is commonly attached to Grant. In his deposition, Grant attested to Babcock's overall faithfulness and efficiency in carrying out his duties, and he added that his secretary had never spoken to him about the charges against the Whiskey Ring or tried to influence him in any way.[141] (Unless one is prepared to concur in McFeely's baseless, though novel, theory—that "Ulysses Grant knew that Orville Babcock was guilty and yet went so far as to perjure himself before the chief justice of the United States to keep his aide out of jail"[142]—historians should consider more seriously the implications of this statement.) However influential this deposition was in the trial, it was not decisive

---

[137] Hesseltine, p. 377.
[138] Nevins, p. 764.
[139] Hesseltine, pp. 377-78.
[140] Coolidge, p. 481; Hesseltine, p. 385.
[141] Hesseltine, p. 387; Coolidge, pp. 483-84.
[142] McFeely, p. 415.

in Babcock's acquittal.[143]   As even condemnatory studies of the Grant administration admit, there was never enough evidence to prove Babcock's guilt.[144]

The impression offered by the traditional consensus that Babcock's guilt was self-evident suggests again the predisposition of historians to believe Grant's enemies.   Given the striking lack of evidence that Babcock, however indiscreet he generally might have been,[145] conspired to cover up the Whiskey Ring, one must rely almost entirely on intuitive judgments to be morally persuaded of his guilt.[146] Relevant to this case, however, is the questionable impetus for the Babcock trial and the weakness of evidence against him.   While it might reasonably be asked whether Grant needlessly lowered his public support by making a deposition, his action was followed by no measurable reaction of this kind.   At the time, in fact, rumors of a rift between Grant and Bristow received considerably more attention than the deposition, and the president's ongoing support of the stringent prosecution of the ring persisted through Babcock's indictment.   The *New York Times* was able to report in its top story one week after Grant's deposition "a continuance of the hearty co-operation of the

---

[143]   Coolidge, p. 484.

[144]   Nevins, p. 802.

[145]   From the start of Grant's presidency, Babcock was the target of charges of involvement in other shady deals. Hesseltine, p. 387; Coolidge, p. 475. Most of these charges appear to be unsupported, but soon after the Whiskey Ring trial, Babcock was indicted for complicity in a safe burglary case, which involved a conspiracy that trumped a burglary charge against a Washington reformer in order to injure him; he later would be acquitted. Boynton, pp. 404-06, 443-46; Hesseltine, p. 395; Nevins, p. 767. Indiscretions often could lie behind even unsupported charges, and this study does not preclude the conclusion that Babcock was indiscreet.   Despite the enthusiasm of the administration's friends for the acquittal, including a drive to raise Babcock's legal expenses, Grant seems to have come to mistrust Babcock's discretion. Hesseltine, p. 387; Nevins, pp. 803, 817-18. After an hour-long discussion between the president and his secretary, Babcock left Grant's household permanently. Hesseltine, p. 388.

[146]   For example, although evidence to prove Babcock's guilt has never been shown, Hesseltine makes the unwarranted inference that Babcock's lawyers' attempts to prevent the introduction of evidence was motivated by the guilt of their client. Hesseltine, p. 387.

President in the Secretary's fight with the whisky thieves."[147] Bristow himself became an unsuccessful candidate for the Republican nomination for president in 1876, and he resigned as Secretary of the Treasury on June 17, the day Hayes won the nomination, causing newspapers to suspect that "after the nomination in Cincinnati he had no further object in remaining in the Treasury."[148]

4. Proceeding to the fourth category of "real" corruption, well-founded charges against Grant's principal subordinates, one finds only the case of the Belknap bribery. The Secretary of War's first wife had agreed to secure an appointment for a New Yorker named Caleb P. Marsh to a lucrative Indian post tradership and to share with him in the profits he made. Marsh then made an agreement with the trading post's incumbent, John S. Evans, to receive $12,000 annually not to take the position. Half of this sum was to be sent to Mrs. Belknap, but she soon died, and the money was then paid to Belknap himself, who eventually used it to support his second wife, the sister of the first.[149] On March 2, 1876, just as information about the scandal was being uncovered in Congress, an upset Belknap went to Grant at the White House and resigned on the spot. Grant accepted the resignation, not having been informed about the situation,[150] and as Belknap exited the White House, Senators Lot M. Morrill and Oliver P. Morton entered to give the president his first piece of information on the impeachment proceedings against Belknap, which would begin later that day. Apart from the impeachment proceedings, Grant ordered Pierrepont to prosecute Belknap, but this failed to bring an indictment.[151]

It certainly would have been preferable, if not feasible, for Grant to have kept Belknap in the cabinet against his will for the sake of the impeachment proceedings by rejecting his resignation. As the situation stood, Belknap was not convicted only because the Senate, a two-thirds

---

[147] *New York Times*, Feb. 25, 1876, p. 1. See generally *New York Times* and *New York Tribune*, Dec. 1875-Feb. 1876. See also Carpenter, p. 151.

[148] Hesseltine, p. 408.

[149] Ibid., p. 395; Nevins, p. 806.

[150] Grant had not heard a word about the case until Bristow called that morning and urged him to speak with Lyman K. Bass, the Buffalo congressman who had been gathering information about Belknap. Grant had a message sent to Bass for an interview at noon, but this meeting had not yet taken place when Belknap entered. Garfield III, pp. 243-44; Hesseltine, p. 395.

[151] Hesseltine, pp. 395-96; Nevins, p. 808; Garfield III, pp. 243-44.

majority of which believed him guilty, doubted its ability to remove a man who had already resigned.[152] Grant's acceptance of Belknap's resignation, however, met with general public approval,[153] and the president's actions provide yet another reason to refute the assertion of the traditional consensus that he naively adhered to corrupt subordinates.

Still, some historians have curiously groped for reasons to condemn Grant in this case, as reflected in the following haphazard explanation offered by Bailey: "When we consider Grant's moral callousness, his insensitivity to graft, his stubborn sympathy for loyal subordinates and benefactors, it is difficult to escape the conclusion that the President was trying his best to help Belknap escape the consequences of his criminality."[154] The fact that Grant made a genuine effort to prosecute Belknap highlights the problematic nature of this assessment. The only criticism that can be levelled against Grant in this case is that resignation should not be accepted as a matter of course, yet even this is not a firmly supported argument when one considers precedent in the many cabinet scandals that preceded the Belknap case as far back as the Washington administration. In fact, when Washington's Secretary of State, Edmund Randolph, was faced with the charge that he had offered to instigate civil strife in America in return for a bribe—a far more serious (though questionable) charge than that which Belknap faced—the matter legally did not proceed beyond Randolph's resignation to Washington.[155]

III.

Although a careful analysis of cases in which charges of corruption were levelled against Grant's subordinates greatly weakens the verdict of the traditional consensus, the third consideration cited previously in assessing the corruption question may prompt historians to ask whether Grant's presidency was not seriously injured even by issues of corruption that did not involve the administration's culpability. That is, it might be asked whether the Belknap bribery or Grant's adherence to certain subordinates who were under fire, even if charges against them

---

[152] Hesseltine, p. 396; Nevins, p. 805.
[153] *New York Times*, Mar. 3, 1876, p. 1.
[154] Bailey, *Presidential Saints and Sinners*, pp. 103-04.
[155] Ibid., p. 8.

were unjustified, did not diminish public confidence in the president— and, in turn, in the prospects for presidential achievement. If Grant had reduced public faith in his own integrity and judgment as a leader by defending certain subordinates who were unattractive to the people, it could justly be viewed, at least in some cases, as the president foolishly imposing political liabilities upon himself.

Such was hardly the case, however. If it were, Grant should have expected public confidence in his honesty and respect for the law to reach its all-time low in 1876, when the Babcock trial and Belknap exposure presented the two greatest potential threats to such confidence. However, Grant's achievement during the electoral crisis of 1876-77, which took place while these events still were fresh in the people's minds, indicates a strikingly different situation. While the electoral crisis, which remains to be discussed, created widespread agitation throughout the country and greatly undermined public confidence in the government, even Hesseltine's condemnatory study admits that it was "the public confidence in" Grant's "honesty," "Grant's character, his popular prestige, and his desire for peace which, as much as any other single factor," brought about a peaceful presidential transition in 1877.[156] Garfield, who was no particular admirer of the president, remarked in October 1876 how Grant's "power of staying" and "imperturbability" had "been of incalculable value to the nation, and will be prized more and more as his career recedes." On the day Grant retired from the presidency, Garfield would be able to write in his diary, "No American has carried greater fame out of the White House than this silent man who leaves it today."[157] Even the traditional consensus does not deny the positive role assumed by Grant during the electoral crisis, though it more often overlooks its broader meaning.

IV.

Comparisons with other administrations, some of which already have been presented, offer a final consideration of the corruption question in Grant's presidency. Soon after Belknap's trial,

---

[156] Hesseltine, pp. 419, 411. See also Carpenter, p. 168.
[157] Garfield III, pp. 366, 454.

Congressman George F. Hoar, a Republican, but not a member of the Grant faction of the party, offered the following observations:

> The Republican Party . . . has controlled the Government for sixteen years, a term equal to that which covers the whole Administration of Washington, the whole Administration of John Adams, and the first term of Jefferson. It has been one of those periods in which all experience teaches us to expect an unusual manifestation of public corruption, of public disorder, and of evils and errors of administration. A great war; the time which follows a great war; great public debts; currency and values inflated; the exertion of new and extraordinary powers for the safety of the State; the sudden call of millions of slaves to a share in the Government—any one of these things would be expected to create great disturbance, and give rise to great temptations and great corruptions. Our term of office has seen them all combined. And yet I do not scruple to affirm that not only has there been less dishonesty and maladministration in the sixteen years of Republican rule proportionally to the numbers and wealth of the people than in the first sixteen years after the inauguration of Washington, but there has been less absolutely of those things.[158]

Coolidge asserts that "it would be absurd to charge" corruption "to Grant or his Administration. The period just following the war was one of rude upheaval and of shattered standards. It cannot fairly be compared with more quiescent times. . . . Another in his place would hardly have done better; a weaker President might have been overwhelmed."[159]   Despite Hoar's observation, it would not be unwarranted to conclude that the post-Civil War era was marked by an unusual amount of corruption.

Historians are hard pressed, however, to demonstrate that the government suffered more from corruption under the Grant administration than under Lincoln and Johnson. Hoogenboom points out that the civil service was at its nadir in 1865, when the spoils system controlled more offices than ever before and the stress of war exposed the deficiencies that came with its unstructured personnel policy.[160]   The era beginning with Grant's presidency saw slow but steady improvement so that

---

[158] Hoar I, p. 310.
[159] Coolidge, p. 430.
[160] Hoogenboom in Morgan, pp. 81-83.

[p]ublic service under Grant was actually more efficient than under Lincoln and Johnson. . . . Although Grant earned the dubious distinction of abandoning civil service reform, no previous president had even experimented with it. Grant was not a civil service reformer, but he was decidedly more interested in reform than his predecessors . . . .[161]

Despite the typical depiction of the age as riddled with malfeasance, it is unlikely that any substantial portion of the federal civil service actually was corrupt or inefficient.[162]

Additionally, as has been pointed out, the two largest of the so-called Grant scandals originated while Johnson was president, and the largest did not even involve activity that took place after Grant's inauguration. Furthermore, while Grant has been widely criticized for poor appointments (usually because they were spoilsmen), it was Johnson whose appointees had unusual records of extravagance;[163] yet this fact tends to be obscured by the political conflict of the Johnson years, which better captures the interest of historians. Amid their preoccupation with the seventeenth president's battle with Congress, historians often forget the Republican platform's declaration in 1868 that Johnson "has perverted the public patronage into an engine of wholesale corruption . . . ."[164]

This is not to say that Johnson should be discredited for the Credit Mobilier, the Whiskey Ring, or the Tweed Ring. As is the case with almost all presidents, appraisals of Johnson do not suffer as the result of the misdeeds of culprits for whose honesty the president could not fairly be held responsible, especially when one looks beyond principal subordinates. In Grant's case, however, historians have allowed literary impressions to supersede the record, and they have painted a portrait of "Grantism" that incorporates all of the real and fabricated evils of the age. "Grossly overrating the organization of satanic spoilsmen, reformers' writings abound with reference to conspiracies and rings,"[165] Hoogenboom points out. Reformers' criticism went

---

[161] Ibid., p. 83.
[162] H. Wayne Morgan, "An Age in Need of Reassessment: A View Beforehand," in Morgan, p. 9.
[163] Hesseltine, p. 136.
[164] *Official Records*, p. 67.
[165] Hoogenboom in Morgan, p. 73.

beyond misappropriating blame; it extended to an outright demonization of their enemies, which has done a great deal to undermine accuracy in history books. Once politics in the 1870's is allowed to be characterized monolithically as a political crusade, it appears to make sense that every disturbing phenomenon that surfaced between 1869 and 1877 is somehow the fault of the villains in power.

While it is true that public confidence in government suffered while Grant was in the White House due to an unusual number of exposures of corruption, this lapse of confidence did not extend to the popular president. In fact, historians might display sounder judgment than the traditional consensus in concluding that a man with Grant's widely recognized honesty, firmness, and respect for the law—not to mention a respectable and unprecedented record in fighting corruption and paving the way toward civil service reform—was the type of leader that was needed in an age of declining faith in public ethics.[166]

"It is traditional to blame the president for the misdeeds of major appointees," asserts Bailey, "including members of the cabinet. Yet this practice is not altogether fair, because the chief executive cannot possibly watch every move of every member of his official family, even a small one, as was Washington's tiny group."[167] It is unfortunate that Bailey applies different standards to Grant. The only substantiated instance of corruption that involved the moral culpability of one of Grant's principal subordinates was the Belknap bribery. (The Sanborn contracts implicated a man who was substantially detached from Grant and concerned the president chiefly as a matter of Secretary Richardson's arguable negligence.) Belknap was hardly a singular case in the long history of cabinet scandals. Had Grant appointed more Belknaps to major positions, it might justify noticeably diminishing his reputation as president, but there is little reason to condemn him for a record that is hardly worse than that of several other presidents whose reputations are virtually unscathed by the corruption issue.

Historians have consistently ranked Harry S Truman among the top ten presidents in the category of "near-greats,"[168] but here seems to lie another historiographical problem. In *The Truman Scandals* (1956), Jules Abels asserts that the cases of corruption during the Grant

---

[166] See Carpenter, p. 168.

[167] Bailey, *Presidential Saints and Sinners*, p. 8.

[168] Murray and Blessing, pp. 16-17.

administration were "very small compared with the corruption which took place in the administration of Harry S. Truman. Never had there been so much corruption practiced by so many public officials in so many different places."[169] While Grant responded "keenly" to disclosures of corruption, Abels charges Truman with "protecting the wrongdoers" in some cases, even to the point that his administration assumed "the shape of a general conspiracy to obstruct justice . . . ."[170] Indeed, even if Abels exaggerates his claims, the issue of inconsistencies between assessments of Grant and those of other presidents is a rich enough topic that an entire volume probably could be devoted to it.

In summary, whether one looks at the weakness of the reformers' charges or the analysis of specific cases by the traditional consensus, it must be concluded that historians have not been justified in assessing the Grant administration as if it were uniquely deserving of the stigma of corruption. To reach this conclusion does not require the invention of novel analytical techniques or a revisionist approach to the entire field of presidential history. To the contrary, this conclusion attempts merely to adjust the standards under which Grant is appraised to fit those of other presidencies.

The weakness of the traditional consensus' charge of corruption, however, is by itself an insufficient explanation of the political situation during Grant's time. Additional dimensions of Grant's years in the White House need to be considered.

---

[169] Abels, pp. 311-12.
[170] Ibid., pp. 310, 314-15.

IV

A RECORD OF INEFFECTIVENESS? THE FORGOTTEN DIMENSION OF GRANT'S PRESIDENCY

While the traditional consensus has been engrossed in demonstrating that corruption was the preeminent feature of the Grant presidency, Coolidge's frequently overlooked study raises the question of emphasis. What Coolidge finds worthy of primary emphasis is the wide range of Grant's achievements in both the domestic and foreign realms, but the traditional consensus has operated on a different wavelength. Nevins casually refers to Grant's "political bankruptcy," and others have dismissed "the barren plain that is Grant's Presidency" as merely "eight long years of scandal."[171] "He had no program with popular appeal and he developed no enemies who would confirm his leadership," asserts Tugwell, yet Coolidge contends that "[n]o programme was ever more faithfully carried out by any President" than Grant's.[172] A look at the record indicates how impoverished traditional analyses have been merely in recognizing and evaluating basic policy matters during the Grant administration.

Grant pursued an economic policy that was singularly successful in the aftermath of the most serious fiscal problems the nation had ever faced. Under his administration, policies were pursued that reduced inflation, bolstered recovery from the mild depression of 1867-69, promoted economy in federal expenditures, and substantially raised the nation's credit.[173] Both taxes and the national debt were reduced during

---

[171] Nevins, p. 811; Magrath, p. 20; Bailey, *Presidential Greatness*, p. 42.

[172] Tugwell, p. 232; Coolidge, p. 527.

[173] Benedict, p. 368; Coolidge, pp. 528, 530; Boutwell, *Reminiscences* II, p. 228.

Grant's presidency by approximately $300 million and $435 million respectively; one-fifth of the national debt had been eliminated, and during Grant's first year in office, Boutwell had successfully established a policy that (if it had been desirable to continue rather than reducing taxation) actually would have paid off the entire national debt in less than a quarter-century.[174] Annual interest rates were reduced by approximately $30 million under Grant's policies, and the balance of trade was changed from over $130 million against the United States to over $120 million in the nation's favor.[175]

Perhaps more significantly, Grant successfully secured the resumption of specie payments. The Resumption Act of 1875 was the culmination of a series of events, decisively affected by Grant's veto of the 1874 inflation bill, that made the Republicans the party of hard money, and while Coolidge praises this, to Hesseltine Grant simply "became the 'safe' representative of the more reactionary economic interests of his day."[176] With the notable exception of Coolidge, the few twentieth-century historians who have explored Grant's economic policy have generally expressed contempt toward the president's course despite its striking success, which raises yet another question of bias among scholars.

Hoogenboom theorizes that

> the historian dislikes the dominant forces in the Gilded Age. The historian is usually liberal, more often than not a Democrat. . . . The post-Civil War era stands for all the historian opposes. It was an era of Republicanism, of big business domination, of few and ineffectual attempts at government regulation, of weak executives, and of an essentially nonprofessional civil service. The historian naturally dwells upon the shortcomings of the period . . . .

Grant's "political career both personifies all the historian abhors and symbolizes Gilded Age politics"[177] according to Hoogenboom, and it is not difficult to see why historians have behaved like eager partisan converts of Grant's enemies. Between Grant's alliance with spoilsmen and his embodiment of Republicanism, he has fallen victim to

---

[174] Richardson IX, p. 4355; Boutwell, *Reminiscences* II, p. 228.

[175] Richardson IX, p. 4355; Hesseltine, p. 417.

[176] Coolidge, p. 453; Hesseltine, p. viii.

[177] Hoogenboom in Morgan, p. 71.

professional bias on more than one front. It is important to recognize the baggage that historians bring with them when they assess their subjects, for it affects the finished product.

Hesseltine sees in the Grant administration the transition of the Republican Party from an organization that had "embodied the dreams of the common man for free land" into one where "professional politicians ran it to serve the interests of conservative business men."[178] Hesseltine's analysis of economic issues under Grant often reads like partisan appraisals of Republicanism that carry into the twentieth century, and Nevins and McFeely display the same trait.[179] The latter author remarks that from the date of Grant's veto of the inflation bill, the Republican Party became "the party not of the working class but of those who were or aspired to be the capitalists."[180] Certainly, Hesseltine, Nevins, and McFeely are all men whose ideologies, like those of most historians, depart substantially from the economic tradition that developed under Grant. (In fact, at the time his landmark study of Grant's presidency was being published, Hesseltine, an active socialist, was warning a colleague that "'the signs and the portents [were] on all sides' that fascism was coming."[181]) McFeely admits that he regards monetary policy as "the dullest of subjects,"[182] and his oversimplification of that complex issue helps demonstrate his attitude.[183]

The dramatic impact of the Resumption Act, which provided for the resumption of specie payments as of January 1, 1879, has eluded every major study of the Grant presidency. The act was "a significant achievement in the opinion of most contemporaries"[184]—one that helped more than just big business—and Resumption Day in 1879 gave rise to the abrupt end of the depression following the Panic of 1873, one of the most severe depressions in the nation's history—about as

---

[178] "Grant's Administration came in a period of transition, while the party was passing from its earlier ideal of preserving the Union into the long period when its goal was protection of the economic interests of Big Business." Hesseltine, p. 372.

[179] Nevins, p. 288; McFeely, p. 397.

[180] McFeely, p. 397.

[181] Novick, pp. 245, 242.

[182] McFeely, p. 320.

[183] McPherson, p. 364.

[184] Benedict, p. 376.

sharp a positive turn in the economy as the nation has ever seen at the end of a depression (see chart). The thorough preparation for resumption up to Resumption Day, which continued after the Grant administration thanks in part to the cooperation of the Hayes administration through Secretary of the Treasury John Sherman, assured the country of the success of the policy, and *Appleton's Annual Cyclopædia* reported the following about the effect of resumption in 1879:

> [A]fter much labor and sacrifice, the country was lifted out of the financial bog of depreciated paper currency, and with the resumption thus happily secured came a revival of business, an extraordinary demand for labor of all kinds, and a confirmation of that confidence which was so necessary for all business enterprises, and which had grown step by step with every movement made toward a specie basis.[185]

Although it occupies relatively little attention, most scholars see as Grant's greatest presidential achievement the settlement of the *Alabama* claims dispute with Great Britain in 1871, which (among other things) both prevented war and settled for the first time in American history every standing border dispute (except that of recently acquired Alaska). John Bassett Moore, one of the foremost experts in international law of his time, calls the Treaty of Washington, which settled the crisis and awarded the United States $15,500,000 in damages through the international tribunal it established in Geneva, "the greatest treaty of actual and immediate arbitration the world had even seen . . . ." Among all of the treaties in American history, he ranks it second only to the peace treaty with Great Britain that acknowledged U.S. independence.[186] The settlement opened a new era in Anglo-American relations and settled a menacing dispute with Canada over fishery rights.

---

[185] "Resumption of Specie Payments," p. 768.

[186] John Bassett Moore, Introduction, in Nevins, p. xv. George S. Boutwell ranked the treaty third in importance in U.S. history, behind the treaty of alliance with France in 1778 and the peace treaty with Great Britain in 1783. Boutwell, *The Lawyer, the Statesman, and the Soldier*, p. 165.

Hesseltine's study contemptuously places discussion of the *Alabama* claims dispute within a chapter entitled "Smoke Screen" (pp. 220-37), which mischaracterizes Grant's foreign policy activity as a way to divert attention from supposed domestic failures.

American Business Activity before and after the Resumption of Specie Payments

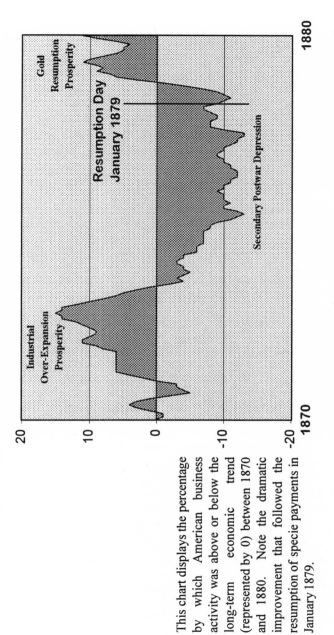

This chart displays the percentage by which American business activity was above or below the long-term economic trend (represented by 0) between 1870 and 1880. Note the dramatic improvement that followed the resumption of specie payments in January 1879.

Source: KeyCorp, "American Business Activity from 1790 to Today," 59th ed., January 1988.

More importantly, however, it established the principle of international arbitration in disputes between countries involving weighty matters of honor.[187]   Grant recognized the importance of the Geneva Arbitration, and upon visiting Geneva after his presidency, he asserted that that city was "where the principle of international arbitration was established, which I hope will be resorted to by other nations and be the means of continuing peace to all mankind."[188]   He had elaborated his vision in a bit more detail before the Midland International Arbitration Union in England, becoming one of the earliest world leaders to advocate the idea of a world congress:[189]

> [N]othing would afford me greater happiness than to know, as I believe will be the case, that, at some future day, the nations of the earth will agree upon some sort of congress, which shall take cognizance of international questions of difficulty, and whose decisions will be as binding as the decision of our Supreme Court is binding on us. It is a dream of mine that some such solution may be found for all questions of difficulty that may arise between different nations.[190]

As the motivating principle behind the Hague Conferences of 1899 and 1907, the League of Nations, the World Court, and the United Nations, international arbitration would be of almost inestimable importance in modern history.[191]   A crucial component of any complete account of peacemaking efforts that followed, the success of the Geneva Arbitration triggered an ongoing movement to seek alternatives to war and to codify international law in order to mitigate the effects of war when it occurred.[192]   It is unfortunate that Grant's positive legacy has not been recognized beyond his warmaking abilities, because history has failed to capture a large part of the picture.

Grant's peacemaking efforts extend to two other crises that brought the U.S. to the brink of war. In June 1870, Grant successfully resisted popular and congressional sentiment for intervention in the Cuban rebellion with a proclamation announcing strict neutrality, a policy for which the administration was especially indebted to the influence of

---

[187] Scaturro, pp. 107-08.
[188] Young, *Around the World* I, p. 50.
[189] Coolidge, p. 311.
[190] Young, *Around the World* I, p. 120.
[191] Nevins, pp. 887, 448; Coolidge, p. 311.
[192] Scaturro, pp. 105, 107-08.

Secretary Fish.[193]   After the *Virginius* affair, to which Hesseltine devotes only one paragraph, again threatened war with Spain in 1873, Grant secured a peaceful settlement along with an indemnity and an apology from Spain.[194] In 1875, the administration additionally secured a commercial reciprocity treaty with Hawaii[195] that forged a path toward eventual annexation.

The president's commitment to peace extended within American borders. On the eve of what could have become the complete genocide of American Indians, Grant initiated his "Quaker" Indian Peace Policy, which established Indian wards and made the government accountable for the welfare of Indians as individuals for the first time in American history.[196]   To a greater extent than any of his predecessors, Grant pointed out the injustice to which the Indians had been subjected and pleaded for reform to curb impending extermination.[197]   His policy

---

[193]   Nevins, pp. 360, 447.

[194]   Ibid., pp. 667-94; Hesseltine, pp. 302-03.

[195]   Richardson IX, p. 4289.

[196]   Rushmore, pp. 65, 68, 75-76.

[197]   See, e.g., Richardson VIII, p. 3992 ("From the foundation of the Government to the present the management of the original inhabitants of this continent—the Indians—has been a subject of embarrassment and expense, and has been attended with continuous robberies, murders, and wars. From my own experience upon the frontiers and in Indian countries, I do not hold either legislation or the conduct of the whites who come most in contact with the Indian blameless for these hostilities."); ibid., p. 3993 ("A system which looks to the extinction of a race is too horrible for a nation to adopt without entailing upon itself the wrath of all Christendom and engendering in the citizen a disregard for human life and the rights of others, dangerous to society."); ibid. IX, p. 4176 ("Wars of extermination, engaged in by people pursuing commerce and all industrial pursuits, are expensive even against the weakest people, and are demoralizing and wicked. Our superiority of strength and advantages of civilization should make us lenient toward the Indian. The wrong inflicted upon him should be taken into account and the balance placed to his credit. The moral view of the question should be considered and the question asked, Can not the Indian be made a useful and productive member of society by proper teaching and treatment? If the effort is made in good faith, we will stand better before the civilized nations of the earth and in our own consciences for having made it."); Keller, p. 25 ("I do not believe our Creator ever placed the different races of men on this earth with a view of having the stronger exert all his energies in exterminating the weaker."). See also Richardson VIII, p. 3962.

provided the impetus for an ongoing government effort to enact Indian reform measures in future decades that eventually culminated in the Indians' citizenship.[198]

Grant's role in the disputed Hayes-Tilden election, which gave rise to the most critical presidential electoral crisis in the nation's history, further demonstrated the president's commitment to peace within the country. The dispute over the 1876 election returns that were to decide the next president instigated many threats of violence and widespread concern over whether the peaceful inauguration of a new president would occur in 1877. In the face of general confusion, Grant, resisting partisan pressure to avoid taking steps that might lead to Democrat Samuel J. Tilden's election, pushed through Congress a bill establishing an electoral commission to determine who won the election, urging the measure as an assurance that the nation would avoid civil war.[199] Faced with threats of violence, Grant quietly strengthened forces around Washington to preserve order, and while many accused him of acting to install Hayes, James G. Blaine observed the decisive role of the president's "good judgment, his cool temperament, and his known courage" in alleviating popular unrest. "No greater proof of General Grant's power to command was given, even on the battle-field, than the quieting effect of his measures upon the refractory and dangerous elements that would have been glad to disturb the public peace," Blaine concluded.[200]

In view of Grant's record, it is curious that Nevins would assert (and credit himself with discovering) that "no other" presidential administration "has closed in such paralysis and discredit as (in all domestic fields) did Grant's," that Grant "was without policies or popular support."[201] Even if one overlooks Garfield's observation that Grant carried unprecedented fame out of the White House, the 1876-77 electoral crisis indicates serious analytical problems behind Nevins' conclusion. The crisis deprived Grant of a true "lame-duck" period; the election results were announced only two days before his term expired, and the crisis itself continued until Hayes was peacefully inaugurated. That Grant's firm policy and popular support played the role it did in

---

[198] Rushmore, p. 76.
[199] Hesseltine, pp. 410-11, 418-19; Nevins, p. 855.
[200] Blaine II, p. 582.
[201] Nevins, p. 811.

that crisis suggests that the opposite of Nevins' assertion might be more accurate.

Despite Grant's record of achievement, which so far has been presented only in part, there persists a strong tradition in the spirit of Nevins which asserts that Grant was a weak executive—that he had few substantive policies, allowed himself to be controlled by Congress, and brought the presidency to perhaps its lowest ebb rather than expanding the powers of the chief executive.[202] This assessment displays a curious tendency to overlook the record in favor of the traditional inclination to dismiss Grant as an ineffective political leader substantially because of his background and apparent character traits. Political scientists Sidney M. Milkis and Michael Nelson go as far as to assert "Grant's virtual abdication of presidential responsibility" and believe that Grant lacked "the political experience a president needs to bend other leaders to his purposes." "Grant considered himself to be purely an administrative officer," and he was "disposed to accept without question the work of Congress as the authoritative expression of the will of the American people."[203]

Grant entered office facing a powerful Senate that had given Congress an unprecedented degree of dominance over the executive, a dominance that was substantially secured by Johnson's impeachment. Many historians and political scientists assert that for decades, the Senate oligarchy continued to dominate the government, and Grant is often perceived as among the most deferential of the presidents between Abraham Lincoln and Theodore Roosevelt.[204] "In Grant," assert Milkis and Nelson, "unlike Lincoln or Johnson, congressional Republicans had a president whom they could manage."[205] Grant's own words actually contribute to such impressions. Coming from a Whig background,[206] Grant often used deferential rhetoric. Upon accepting the Republican nomination for the presidency in 1868, he referred to his future position as that of "a purely Administrative officer" who, rather than committing himself to a policy to follow for four years when issues and public views were constantly changing, "should always be left free to execute the will of the people. I always have respected that will, and always

---

[202] See Rossiter, pp. 30-33.
[203] Milkis & Nelson, pp. 165-67.
[204] See Bailey, *Presidential Greatness*, p. 296.
[205] Milkis & Nelson, p. 166.
[206] Young, *Around the World* II, p. 268.

shall."[207]   In his First Inaugural Address, he asserted, "I shall, on all subjects, have a policy to recommend, but none to enforce against the will of the people."[208]   A lack of familiarity with the events that followed might easily lead one to misinterpret President Grant, for his actions infer that he had a stronger attitude about executive leadership than his rhetoric implies.

Upon entering office, as has been seen, Grant displayed striking independence from Congress; his subsequent decision to involve congressmen on matters of patronage, however, marked not a surrender to the legislative branch, but a step toward influencing them in directions that would be conducive to policy successes.   Grant announced to his cabinet "his determination to hold members of the party to the support of the policy of his Administration," and the extent of the control he exerted over both department heads and Congress often seemed unorthodox, particularly by the standards of the nineteenth century.[209]   The *New York Tribune* observed that "no President has ever made his Cabinet merely so many staff officers."[210] Although he allowed his cabinet considerable freedom in running their departments, he expected from them the strictest subordination that paralleled his previous expectations of military staff members.   When asked why Secretary of the Interior Cox resigned from the cabinet, Grant replied, "The trouble was that General Cox thought the Interior Department was the whole government, and that Cox was the Interior Department. I had to point out to him in very plain language that there were three controlling branches of the government, and that I was the head of one of these, and would like so to be considered by the Secretary of the Interior."[211]   "No man being conspicuous" in his cabinet, Hayes approvingly observed, "Grant's leadership and rule is beyond question."[212]

Not all contemporary politicians shared such views.   Senator John Sherman expressed regret that Grant "regarded these heads of departments . . . as mere subordinates, whose functions he might assume" and attributed this view to the president's misunderstanding of

---

[207]   Grant, *Papers* XVIII, p. 264.
[208]   Ibid. XIX, p. 139. See also Richardson VIII, p. 3960.
[209]   Hesseltine, p. 254; Nevins, pp. 364-65.
[210]   Hesseltine, p. 138.
[211]   Garland, p. 427.
[212]   Williams III, p. 59.

"the true theory of our government."[213] "[I]f he erred, it was from a want of experience in the complicated problems of our form of government. The executive department of a republic like ours should be subordinate to the legislative department. The President should obey and enforce the laws, leaving to the people the duty of correcting any errors committed by their representatives in Congress."[214] Sherman concluded that the "limitation of the power of the President" over cabinet members "is one that an army officer, accustomed to give or receive orders, finds it difficult to understand and to observe when elected President."[215]

It is interesting that different commentators could draw such diverging conclusions about a president's exercise of power based upon his lack of experience in politics. The unorthodox nature of the control Grant exerted possibly did stem in part from the limits of his political training, but it also should be understood that Grant was an innovator by nature who refused to be a slave to convention. He had become a general after receiving a considerable amount of military training, yet his transcendent generalship displayed a departure from convention that allowed him to make his mark as perhaps the first of the world's modern generals and as a principal innovator of modern warfare. Similarly, Grant's willingness to break with custom helped make him an unusually strong president. It was Grant who provided the impetus for those legislative achievements that have been cited so far in this study, and the president either initiated or otherwise played a decisive role in achievements regarding Reconstruction that remain to be explored. His means for securing desirable legislative results were not always conventional, and Coolidge, whose appraisal of Grant is generally laudatory, nevertheless saw it as a fault that he engaged in "the practice, which he carried to a greater length than any of his predecessors, of interfering with congressional affairs."[216]

It is difficult to adhere to the notion of Grant's surrender to Congress when one considers his response to the only one of his major goals to be defeated by Congress: the annexation of Santo Domingo. It was Charles Sumner, chairman of the Senate Foreign Relations Committee and the nation's most prestigious senator, who secured the

---

[213] Sherman I, p. 449.
[214] Ibid., p. 447.
[215] Ibid., pp. 449-50.
[216] Coolidge, p. 428.

defeat of Grant's annexation treaty, and he also posed a serious threat to the success of the more critical *Alabama* claims resolution.[217] Angered by what he perceived as Sumner's dishonesty and insubordination, determined to enforce party discipline, and hoping for success in the negotiations with Great Britain, Grant, behaving like anything but a deferential executive, demanded that legislators unseat him as chairman. Sumner was deposed accordingly, and Simon Cameron, a strong supporter of the president, was installed as the new Foreign Relations Committee chairman in time for Grant to have an uncompromised success with the Treaty of Washington in the Senate.[218] Sumner thus was not to play the role with the Treaty of Washington that Henry Cabot Lodge would play with the League of Nations.[219]

Having assumed office on the heels of a president who had had a majority of his vetoes overturned,[220] Grant restored the effective use of the veto, employing it 93 times—more than all of his predecessors combined.[221] (Only four of these vetoes were overturned, and one of those instances came at the president's request after reassessing the veto.[222]) The most important of these vetoes was that of the 1874 inflation bill, a decisive reversal of the economic course set by Congress that would be followed by the passage of the Resumption Act at Grant's urging, which in turn made him "the President most responsible for putting this country on a gold standard."[223] For Grant's supporters, his veto achieved "the victory of the national credit."[224] Inflationists were annoyed at their defeat, and although they wished to move to override the veto, they had little choice but to heed the reminder of Blaine, the Speaker of the House, of "Charles Sumner's

---

[217] Nevins, pp. 449, 440-41, 459, 463-64.
[218] Hesseltine, pp. 234, 236, 250.
[219] Scaturro, p. 42; Nevins, p. 464.
[220] Senate Library, p. 30.
[221] Ibid., pp. ix, 38.
[222] Ibid., pp. 38, 42, 51-52; Jackson, pp. 148, 133. Carlton Jackson concludes from Grant's veto record that "at least in some respects, he may be considered to have been a powerful Executive. Any Chief Executive who gave forty-four regular vetoes and about the same amount of pocket vetoes, while Congress overrode only three of them, was not a weak president." Jackson, p. 148. Jackson's count of Grant's vetoes at 94 with only three overridden, ibid., pp. viii, 148, differs somewhat from the Senate Library's current numbers.
[223] Jackson, pp. 135-37.
[224] Young, *Men and Memories* II, p. 465.

fate three years before when he had crossed Grant."[225] The president gave a variety of reasons for vetoing different bills, and some vetoes were justified with arguments zealously protecting presidential prerogative and resisting congressional encroachments.[226]

In 1873, Grant became the first president to request the power to exercise a line-item veto, and he initiated the first formal discussion of the issue between Congress and the chief executive in American history.[227] In 1876, Grant approved a rivers and harbors bill that was padded with many riders, but he established a new presidential prerogative by refusing to spend treasury funds on several of the bill's appropriations, arguing that they were "for works of purely private or local interest, in no sense national."[228] Recognizing the limitations that faced the chief executive without the line-item veto, Grant thus started the presidential practice of impoundment and "established what from a modern President's point of view is the argument at the heart of the impoundment issue."[229]

In view of the evidence, whether it be Grant's achievements or his unusually strong, precedent-setting record in dealing with Congress, it must be concluded that traditional notions of Grant's weakness as a chief executive are simply inaccurate. Benedict observes as few have that Grant "dominated his era, a stronger president than most have recognized,"[230] but most historians continue to see him as the least worthy of America's forgettable presidents: "Between Lincoln and Theodore Roosevelt," writes Bailey, "we find . . . eight rather ordinary men, except for the subordinary Grant."[231] Declaring Grant the most underrated figure in American history, David H. Donald asserts to the contrary that "the evidence shows" that Grant was "a skillful and successful politician."[232] Indeed, the stage is set for what would promise to be a fiery debate among historians, if only more scholars were to revisit the Grant presidency. Many complex questions have

---

[225] Jackson, p. 137.

[226] Ibid., pp. 139-40.

[227] "Impoundment," p. 22.

[228] Ibid., pp. 22-23; Richardson IX, p. 4331.

[229] "Impoundment," p. 22.

[230] Benedict, p. 377.

[231] Bailey, *Presidential Greatness*, p. 101.

[232] "Overrated and Underrated Americans," p. 52.

been considered so far, but there remains to be explored one primary facet of President Grant's era that reshapes the entire debate.

V

RECONSTRUCTION

A. Historiographical Prelude

The fact that Grant's administration extended through the last eight years of Reconstruction has spurred curiously little attention from historians of the post-Civil War era. The vast majority of Reconstruction studies focus upon the turbulent age of Johnson, which offers a more dramatic political conflict within the federal government than the Grant years. The issue of Reconstruction, however, sheds new light on the entire political situation during Grant's time. As has been suggested previously, there is more to the reformers than civil service reform, just as there is more to Grant's supporters than patronage. In order to understand the reformers—and, in turn, to understand a major oversight of the traditional consensus in evaluating President Grant— one must recognize the circumstances under which they came into existence as an organized group dedicated specifically to defeating Grant in 1872 through the Liberal Republican Party.

At the center of the Reconstruction debate stood over four million slaves whose status became a matter of domestic dispute surpassed in magnitude only by the war itself. Initially, Johnson's program of Reconstruction had fostered among many former Confederates the hope of precluding the political advancement of Southern blacks, but this hope was displaced in 1867 by Radical Reconstruction. Events subsequent to military rule in the South tend to appear hazy in history after Grant entered the White House. This is unfortunate, for the articulation of Grant's views on the former slaves and the

implementation of his Reconstruction policies are unique components
of the struggle to include Black Americans in the broad plan of
American democracy.   While Lyndon B. Johnson currently receives
more attention than any other president for his racial record—some of
this attention due undoubtedly to "presentism"—Grant frequently acted
on racial issues on a larger scale and in the face of greater resistance.

"I would like to see truthful history written," Grant wrote in his
Personal Memoirs. ". . . For the present, and so long as there are living
witnesses of the great war of sections, there will be people who will not
be consoled for the loss of a cause which they believed to be holy. As
time passes, people, even of the South, will begin to wonder how it was
possible that their ancestors ever fought for or justified institutions
which acknowledged the right of property in man."[233] However, Grant
probably would have been disappointed in the history that followed his
death.   In his far-sighted study of Reconstruction, W.E.B. DuBois
observed in 1935 (the year Hesseltine's book was published):

> The treatment of the period of Reconstruction reflects small credit upon
> American historians as scientists.   We have too often a deliberate
> attempt so to change the facts of history that the story will make
> pleasant reading for Americans. . . .
>
> War and especially civil strife leave terrible wounds. It is the duty
> of humanity to heal them. It was therefore soon conceived as neither
> wise nor patriotic to speak of all the causes of strife and the terrible
> results to which sectional differences in the United States had led. And
> so, first of all, we minimized the slavery controversy which convulsed
> the nation from the Missouri Compromise down to the Civil War. On
> top of that, we passed by Reconstruction with a phrase of regret or
> disgust. . . .
>
> Not a single great leader of the nation during the Civil War and
> Reconstruction has escaped attack and libel. . . . We have been cajoling
> and flattering the South and slurring the North, because the South is
> determined to re-write the history of slavery and the North is not
> interested in history but in wealth. . . .
>
> What is the object of writing the history of Reconstruction? Is it to
> wipe out the disgrace of a people which fought to make slaves of
> Negroes? Is it to show that the North had higher motives than freeing
> black men? Is it to prove that Negroes were black angels? No, it is
> simply to establish the Truth, on which Right in the future may be built.
> We shall never have a science of history until we have in our colleges

---

[233] Grant, *Personal Memoirs* I, p. 170.

men who regard the truth as more important than the defense of the white race, and who will not deliberately encourage students to gather thesis material in order to support a prejudice or buttress a lie. . . .

The most magnificent drama in the last thousand years of human history is the transportation of ten million human beings out of the dark beauty of their mother continent into the new-found Eldorado of the West. They descended into Hell; and in the third century they arose from the dead, in the finest effort to achieve democracy for the working millions which this world had ever seen. . . . Yet we are blind and led by the blind. . . . [I]n a day when the human mind aspired to a science of human action, a history and psychology of the mighty effort of the mightiest century, we fell under the leadership of those who would compromise with truth in the past in order to make peace in the present and guide policy in the future.[234]

William A. Dunning effectively formulated the traditional verdict on Grant and Reconstruction in the early 1900's: "Grant in 1868 had cried peace, but in his time, with the radicals and carpet-baggers in the saddle, there was no peace; with Hayes peace came."[235] As long as the Dunning school remained dominant, with its view of Reconstruction as a misguided failure, historians generally did not hesitate to assert Grant's devotion to the program. Edwin C. Woolley of the Dunning school condemned Grant for his stubborn insistence that the "Fourteenth and Fifteenth amendments applied to the whole Union, and must be enforced equally throughout the Union . . . regardless of consequences, established law must be obeyed. Grant could see no other way." Woolley praised those Republicans who "did see another way," who "saw that it was impossible to continue in Grant's way," as "more practical, more flexible than the President . . . ."[236] Even Coolidge, who concluded that Grant's presidency ranks second to Washington's in constructive achievements, asked his readers to "except the baneful Southern problem . . . where his fault, if fault there was, lay in the rigid execution of the law . . . ."[237] In 1954, Bruce Catton, the preeminent Grant biographer of his time, asserted that

---

[234] DuBois, pp. 713-14, 723, 725, 727.
[235] Current, p. 6.
[236] Woolley, p. 199.
[237] Coolidge, p. 533.

Grant believed that the most important single issue was the reconstruction program. He believed that the sacred heart of that program lay in the effort to protect the Negro in his new freedom. He believed too . . . that the Negro would infallibly be trodden back down into second-class citizenship or worse unless the strong arm of the Federal government protected him.[238]

Catton viewed Reconstruction as a process in which each step brought the policy closer to an undesirable conclusion:

It appeared that the Negro's rights would be insecure unless he had the right to vote, so universal Negro suffrage was decreed. It proved quite simple for Southerners to keep the Negro from the polls by fraud and by violence, and so Federal troops were called on. When Southerners reacted defiantly to such measures, sterner measures were adopted. Step by step, repression took the place of reconciliation . . . .[239]

By remaining as dedicated as he was to Reconstruction, Catton believed that Grant was moved "into a position where the most extreme policy was his policy, and where the most violent partisans claimed him as their leader."[240]

Oddly enough, after the revisionism of the 1960's convinced historians that Reconstruction was actually a noble effort, less has been written about Grant's dedication to it. Only two major studies on point have been written since revisionism—William Gillette's *Retreat from Reconstruction, 1869-1879* (1979) and McFeely's biography—and both question whether Grant truly was committed to protecting the civil and political rights of Southern blacks.[241] McFeely asserts that "the opportunity for Reconstruction was not, in the main, taken" under President Grant and that "[b]y the summer of 1876 there was no one around the White House who gave a damn about the black people."[242] One may ask whether all of these appraisals are intended for the same man; they have little in common except that they criticize their object. Either one or both of these two modes of thought—pre- and post-revisionist critics of Grant's Reconstruction record—fail to apply a fair

---

[238] Catton, p. 179.

[239] Ibid., p. 174.

[240] Ibid., p. 175.

[241] Gillette, pp. 164, 45, 42; McFeely, pp. xii, 439.

[242] McFeely, pp. xii, 439.

historical perspective. They do illustrate once again how impoverished historical discourse becomes when it is difficult to establish the basic facts of a case, the problem that one finds among other issues of the Grant presidency.

B. Grant's First Term: Achievement, Opposition, and the Reformers Revisited

When Grant became president, Congress no longer needed to fear a presidential impediment to Reconstruction, but a Southern white counterrevolution remained as determined as ever not to allow the political advancement of blacks. Military rule remained in only three states—Virginia, Mississippi, and Texas—and Grant's challenge was to protect a new racial order under civil rule in the South in the face of stubborn resistance. The Fourteenth Amendment already had established a national citizenship and replaced the three-fifths compromise, which counted each slave as three-fifths of a person for purposes of representation in the House of Representatives, with a recognition of Black Americans as full citizens. However, the Constitution had yet to insure that blacks could not be denied their voting rights. "The question of suffrage is one which is likely to agitate the public so long as a portion of the citizens of the nation are excluded from its privileges in any state," Grant asserted in his First Inaugural Address. "It seems to me very desirable that the question should be settled now . . . by the ratification of the fifteenth article of amendment to the Constitution."[243]

By December 1869, chances for the ratification of the proposed amendment seemed slim as Congress failed to take a decisive stand on the removal of Georgia's black legislators by the state's Democrats. On December 6, Grant broke the indecision in his First Annual Message. Eager to secure the ratification of the Fifteenth Amendment, the president made an example of Georgia by requesting its temporary return to military rule; Congress complied in sixteen days and required the state to ratify the new amendment.[244] Grant successfully had given white Southerners a warning and helped Reconstruction reach new heights. On March 30, 1870, he departed from presidential custom by

---

[243] Grant, *Papers* XIX, p. 142; Hesseltine, p. 157; Richardson VIII, p. 3962.

[244] Richardson VIII, p. 3982; Gillette, pp. 86-88.

sending an enthusiastic message announcing the ratification of the Fifteenth Amendment:

> A measure which makes at once 4,000,000 people voters who were heretofore declared by the highest tribunal in the land not citizens of the United States, nor eligible to become so (with the assertion that "at the time of the Declaration of Independence the opinion was fixed and universal in the civilized portion of the white race, regarded as an axiom in morals as well as in politics, that black men had no rights which the white man was bound to respect") [a reference to the *Dred Scott* decision], is indeed a measure of grander importance than any other one act of the kind from the foundation of our free Government to the present day. . . . To the race more favored heretofore by our laws I would say, Withhold no legal privilege of advancement to the new citizen. . . . I would therefore call upon Congress to take all the means within their constitutional powers to promote and encourage popular education throughout the country . . . [for] all who possess and exercise political rights . . . .[245]

The initial aim of Grant's Southern policy was conciliatory: he sought to convey to the South a spirit of magnanimity reminiscent of his surrender terms at Appomattox. At the same time, he would not permit what he felt was gained in 1865 to be sacrificed by the suppression of the rights of the black citizen.[246] The intimidation and violence that developed in the South had that very aim, and Grant would demonstrate that political and civil equality was his priority. The traditional charge that Grant was flagrant in his oppression of the South frequently, though unintentionally, attests to this.

Massive racial violence did not permeate the entire South during Grant's presidency. Where the black presence was not a formidable enough political threat to conservatives, as in Virginia, large-scale violence was generally absent.[247] In more turbulent states like South Carolina, Mississippi, and Louisiana, all torn by racial violence, Grant would respond with a controversial series of responses that mark a unique chapter in American history.

---

[245] Richardson VIII, pp. 4009-10. See also Grant, *Papers* XX, pp. 130-31.
[246] Young, *Around the World* II, pp. 359-61.
[247] Gillette, p. 28.

Before analyzing the domestic situation further, Grant's widely misunderstood and unsuccessful attempt in 1870 to annex Santo Domingo deserves mention. Gillette, who merely concludes that "the nation had enough problems without annexing more territory,"[248] fails, as most historians do, to recognize the racial significance of the matter. Nevins summarily asserts that "[t]he Santo Domingo treaty had deserved defeat"[249] without analysis (or even acknowledgment) of the racial issues involved.

During his first year in office, Grant made perhaps the earliest recorded presidential assertion acknowledging the existence of racism as a fundamental problem facing the nation: "The present difficulty, in bringing all parts of the United States to a happy unity and love of country grows out of the prejudice to color. The prejudice is a senseless one, but it exists."[250] (Interestingly enough, the treaty's critics often fell back on racism to bolster their position, deeming the Dominicans unfit for the rights and responsibilities of American citizenship.[251]) Aware of the harshness of racism facing Southern blacks and asserting, "Caste has no foothold in San Domingo,"[252] Grant hoped that after annexation, Santo Domingo would become perhaps three or four additional states. Comprised of black citizens and black state governments, many Southern blacks would find it a refuge "where their civil rights would not be disputed and where their labor would be so much sought after that the poorest among them could have found the means to go."[253]

McFeely incorrectly views this as merely "a segregated settlement,"[254] but Grant in fact sought to use Santo Domingo, in George Sinkler's words, "as a lever or club which the Afro-American could hold over the head of his oppressor in the hope of getting equal rights."[255] "The colored man cannot be spared until his place is supplied," Grant asserted, "but with a refuge like San Domingo his worth here would soon be discovered, and he would soon receive such recognition as to induce him to stay: or if Providence designed that the two races should not live to-gether he would

---

[248] Ibid., p. 56.
[249] Nevins, p. 449.
[250] Grant, *Papers* XX, p. 74.
[251] Foner, pp. 496-97.
[252] Grant, *Papers* XX, p. 74.
[253] Richardson IX, p. 4366.
[254] McFeely, p. 337.
[255] Sinkler, pp. 153-54.

find a home in the Antill[e]s."[256]   Although this statement on its face expresses some bewilderment over whether the two races would be able to live together in harmony, the sum of Grant's recorded statements make it clear that the president was aiming for equal rights, not segregation.[257]   Referring to the "great oppression and cruelty" toward blacks, Grant asserted near the end of his presidency, long after the annexation issue had been settled,

> I do not suppose the whole race would have gone, nor is it desirable that they should go. Their labor is desirable—indispensable almost— where they now are. But the possession of this territory would have left the negro "master of the situation," by enabling him to demand his rights at home on pain of finding them elsewhere.[258]

Unlike Lincoln, Grant left the imperative to migrate in the hands of Providence, believing, as he wrote in his memoirs, that Black Americans were after all "brought to our shores by compulsion" and "now should be considered as having as good a right to remain here as any other class of our citizens."[259]   Meanwhile, plenty of work remained for the president within the country's borders.

The determination of many Southern whites to undermine the Fourteenth and Fifteenth Amendments through intimidation and violence against blacks established the central problem for Grant's Southern policy: enforcement.   The Ku Klux Klan had existed since 1866, but it was not until after the ratification of the Fifteenth Amendment, and in the midst of Grant's frequent declarations of federal support for voting rights, that Congress passed five Enforcement Acts between 1870 and 1872. Designed to prevent state officials from discriminating against voters based on race, they empowered the president to bring cases of conspiracy, fraud, bribery,

---

[256] Grant, *Papers* XX, pp. 74-75. It also should be noted that Grant did not promote annexation without establishing that in fact the people of Santo Domingo desired it. Richardson VIII, p. 4053. Contrast also McFeely's view of the matter as segregationist with Brooks Simpson's view of it as an attempt to "give blacks economic leverage in their struggle to secure equality at home." Simpson, "Butcher?," p. 82.

[257] See Grant, *Papers* XX, pp. 19-20.

[258] Richardson IX, p. 4366. Frederick Douglass offered the plan his strong support. See Douglass IV, pp. 342-45, 354-55, 603-05.

[259] Grant, *Personal Memoirs* II, p. 550; Sinkler, pp. 151, 154.

and intimidation to federal court. Today, these statutes remain the farthest reaching (and most widely litigated) provisions under which a person can realize or vindicate constitutional rights.

The most sweeping of these acts was the Ku Klux Klan Act of April 20, 1871.[260] In March of that year, while responding to a request by the governor of South Carolina for military aid to suppress widespread racial terrorism, Grant had asked Congress to broaden his authority.[261] At the time, he was acting under a broad interpretation of a statute that authorized the suppression of "insurrection;" since he actually was facing crime and violence, he decided that an expansion of his legal power was in order.[262] The Ku Klux Klan Act, passed within one month of Grant's request, brought various crimes committed by individuals against the equal protection of the law within federal jurisdiction for the first time and gave the president the power both to suppress state disorders on his own initiative through military force and to suspend *habeas corpus*.[263] On May 3, Grant called for "acquiescence in the results of" the Civil War, "now written in our Constitution . . . ." He asked the people to help suppress "combinations of lawless and disaffected persons" through their local governments and expressed his own reluctance to exercise his "extraordinary powers" unless there was an "imperative necessity."[264] Nevertheless, he asserted, "I will not hesitate to exhaust the powers . . . vested in the Executive whenever and wherever it shall become necessary" to secure "the peaceful enjoyment of" the constitutional rights of "citizens of every race and color . . . ."[265]

After Attorney General Akerman confirmed that the Klan in South Carolina was out of control, Grant issued a warning proclamation on October 12, 1871, ordering the terrorists to disperse and surrender arms. The warning was ignored, and on October 17, Grant suspended *habeas corpus* in nine South Carolina counties, possibly the boldest display of peacetime presidential power in American history.[266] Soldiers under army officers and United States marshals proceeded to

---

[260] Foner, p. 454.
[261] Richardson IX, pp. 4081-82.
[262] Woolley, pp. 182-83.
[263] Foner, pp. 454-55; Gillette, p. 26.
[264] Richardson IX, pp. 4088-89.
[265] Ibid.
[266] Ibid., p. 4105.

make arrests, and the turbulence ended as Klan atrocities were documented.[267] As Benedict writes,

> the effect was electric. . . . Democrats denounced the imposition of martial law in scattered counties of South Carolina and the use of federal troops elsewhere as gross violations of civil liberty, but they were also forced at last to give up their open hostility to equal rights and black suffrage. Announcing a "new departure," they promised to accept the finality of the Thirteenth, Fourteenth, and Fifteenth amendments.[268]

Within one year of Grant's demonstration in South Carolina, the Ku Klux Klan, practically speaking, was dead,[269] not to reappear until the following century.

One of the weaknesses of Gillette's study is reflected in his verdict that the effort to enforce the Fifteenth Amendment was "pitiable," "badly planned," "brave talk but timid action," "inadequately executed," characterized by "intense partisan interest at every stage," and that such successes as the one in South Carolina were "minor."[270] He backs this extensive criticism with conviction rates under the Enforcement Acts, which amounted to 34% between 1870 and 1877 in the South and which declined after 1873.[271] He points out that the Justice Department generally lacked both money and high-caliber federal officials, but the basis of his argument is substantially confined to bureaucratic criticism and his presumption that the Grant administration had weak, partisan motivations.[272] Had he broadened his outlook, Gillette might have attempted to test his arguments against better historical perspective. While he denounces the Justice Department as the weak instrument of a feeble will, he fails to consider that the infant executive department had been created in 1870 in the most extensive single consolidation of the legal capacity of the federal government up to that time.[273]

Leaving his readers with conclusions that are similar to Gillette's, McFeely contends that "[w]ith Akerman's departure on January 10,

---

[267] McFeely, pp. 369-70; Richardson IX, p. 4105.
[268] Benedict, p. 367.
[269] Woolley, p. 184.
[270] Gillette, pp. 42, 45, 55, 51.
[271] Ibid., p. 42.
[272] Ibid., pp. 31, 54-55.
[273] See McFeely, pp. 368, 424.

1872, went any hope that the Republican party would develop as a national party of true racial equality," and "the new attorney general, George H. Williams, was neither learned nor concerned with much of anything except his career and his exceedingly costly wife."[274] Besides perpetuating old stereotypes of Grant's political cronies, McFeely ignores the dedication and skill with which Williams carried out the prosecution of the Klan. Over three times as many cases were prosecuted in 1872 as in 1871, with almost four times as many convictions. In 1873, four times as many cases were brought as in 1871, and there were again nearly four times more convictions.[275]

Furthermore, the Enforcement Acts were highly controversial both during Reconstruction and for many years after the Supreme Court undermined them in *United States v. Reese* (1876)[276] and *United States v. Cruikshank* (1876),[277] where it struck down provisions of the Enforcement Act of 1870 and narrowly interpreted the Fourteenth and Fifteenth Amendments. Gillette errs in dismissing the political impact of Grant's actions as mere partisanship without realizing that this impact was, in fact, the strength of the act. Greatly susceptible to the politically devastating charge of dictatorship, Grant executed a display of peacetime authority unequaled by either his predecessors or his successors.

Measures as controversial as the Enforcement Acts historically have needed to rely more on political shock waves for success than on the legal statistics they produce. The Alien and Sedition Acts of 1798 and Lincoln's suspension of *habeas corpus* in 1861, neither of which produced conviction statistics even approaching those of the Enforcement Acts, would have failed Gillette's narrow litmus test for effectiveness, yet both relied primarily upon their political impact. Continuing the suppression of civil liberties to the exhaustion of legal potential in such instances is not the task of the president any more than it is desirable or realistic under political constraints. An application of political factors indicates that a president's power is primarily coercive.[278] Legal actions are necessary for coercion, but legal statistics

---

[274] Ibid., pp. 374, 385.

[275] McPherson, p. 364; Gillette, p. 43.

[276] 92 U.S. 214.

[277] 92 U.S. 542.

[278] Compare Foner's observations on the 1871-72 prosecutions: "Judged by the percentage of Klansmen actually indicted and convicted, the fruits of

do not measure either effectiveness or presidential will. Gillette fails to note that Grant's intervention in the South, which often would occur outside the bounds of federal election enforcement, exerted an authority that aimed to alleviate violations of the Fourteenth and Fifteenth Amendments outside legislative mandates. Conviction rates were highest, as might have been expected, when the federal government faced the single greatest threat to political equality: the Ku Klux Klan. Gillette's failure to maintain political perspective is reflected in his departure from his own warning, buried in an endnote: "It has proved easier to measure statistics than to determine their significance."[279] As a result, the "new departure" eludes his study, as well as Eric Foner's observation that by 1872, Grant's willingness to bring the Enforcement Acts' "legal and coercive authority to bear had broken the Klan's back and produced a dramatic decline in violence throughout the South."[280] Historians who have been most responsible for Grant's reputation, however, have been on an entirely different wavelength. For example, Nevins writes in his chapter on the 1872 election that at the time, "To unprejudiced observers, the weakest portion of Grant's record was its Southern chapter."[281]

The Fifteenth Amendment was framed amid great opposition among the states, and ratification required extraordinary effort. It would be an enormous error to disregard the fact that Grant's Southern policy was hindered by the effort to superimpose other priorities on the political agenda at the expense of abandoning Southern blacks. What Gillette regards as a mere "partisan . . . propaganda barrage"[282] was an attempt by Grant and his allies to demonstrate to the people the importance of Southern atrocities as a fundamental issue that had to be faced.[283]

The president's resistance to efforts to superimpose other priorities on the political agenda at Reconstruction's expense incurred costs on his own historical reputation from which he never has recovered. After

---

'enforcement' seem small indeed, a few hundred men among thousands guilty of heinous crimes. But in terms of its larger purposes—restoring order, reinvigorating the morale of Southern Republicans, and enabling blacks to exercise their rights as citizens—the policy proved a success." Foner, p. 458.

[279] Gillette, p. 386.
[280] Foner, pp. 458-59.
[281] Nevins, p. 601.
[282] Gillette, p. 55.
[283] Benedict, p. 367.

the "new departure," despite their professed support for the Fourteenth and Fifteenth Amendments, Democrats attacked the Enforcement Acts that had been passed to uphold them, and they joined reformers in condemning the administration for corruption.[284] Grant's adherence to Reconstruction also created a division within the Republican Party that contributed to the movement by reformers to block his reelection in 1872:

> Reformers lamented the sacrifice of "real" issues, such as tariff and civil-service reform, to the "dead" one symbolized by the "bloody shirt" . . . . Throughout the North, however, Republicans rallied to protect the fruits of Northern victory in the Civil War. . . . The new departure enabled Democrats, reform Republicans, and some Republican politicians who had lost power in their party to unite against Grant's reelection. Calling themselves Liberal Republicans, the dissident Republicans met . . . to frame a platform and name a candidate whom the Democrats would endorse.[285]

Few historians realize that both the birth and the survival of Grant's enemies as a group specifically "centered on attitudes toward Grant himself and the new politics of the Gilded Age" were deeply intertwined with Grant's dedication to Reconstruction. "Fundamentally, reformers believed, Southern violence arose from the same cause as political corruption: the exclusion from office of men of 'intelligence and culture.' . . . [L]iberal reform had come to view Reconstruction as an expression of all the real and imagined evils of the Gilded Age," Foner asserts, and "the rise of the Stalwarts did less to undermine Republican Southern policy than the emergence of an influential group of party reformers whose revolt against the new politics of the Grant era came to include the demand for an end to Reconstruction."[286]

It is the importance of Reconstruction issues during the Grant presidency that has led to a central oversight by the traditional consensus, which assesses the administration as if it were a component strictly of Gilded Age politics. Historians cannot evaluate the Grant administration properly if they separate the politics of the Gilded Age from the politics of Reconstruction. Both were primary features of the

---

[284] Hesseltine, p. 258.
[285] Benedict, p. 367.
[286] Foner, pp. 499, 488.

1870's, and in order to understand Grant's political situation, historians must recognize how fundamental the inconsistency was between the reformers' revered concept of government by the best educated in their elite class and the notion of black rule in the South, the latter being an essential part of Grant's program.

In fact, Nevins asserts that Grant's Southern policy was "[m]ost distressing of all to liberal and moderate observers,"[287] and Sproat points to the central fear of liberals: "that the administration was determined to continue military rule and to subject the 'better elements' in the South to new indignities."[288] Hesseltine refers to "the mass of thinking men" as the people who were "constantly more critical of Grant's conduct" regarding the South, and he uses a parallel form of elitist terminology—"men of property and intelligence"—to refer to the Southern opponents of black rule who were burdened with taxes while carpetbaggers and scalawags had control.[289]

It is revelatory that terms such as the "better elements" and "men of property and intelligence" are used to refer to both elite reformers and opponents of Radical regimes in the South. When viewed in a context that includes Reconstruction, criticisms of Grant's many Radical allies—and, in turn, the charge that the president was a poor judge of character—emerge in a different light. Dunning himself attributed Grant's "adhesion to the radical rather than the moderate Republicans" to "an utter lack of ability to judge men."[290] Most of what Bailey calls "the blowsy, horsy, cigar-smoking crowd that swarmed around him and took full advantage of his befuddlement" were Radicals, and the third-term rumors that worried moderates like Garfield were based largely on the belief that the "crowd of people around" Grant saw the president as the only man who could preserve Reconstruction in the midst of the escalating Southern reaction.[291] The appointment of the largely unknown Akerman fueled distrust of Grant's judgment in selecting appointees, yet since revisionism, Akerman's record in prosecuting racial violence in the South has made him one of the most celebrated attorneys general in American

---

[287] Nevins, p. 289.
[288] Sproat, p. 76.
[289] Hesseltine, pp. 341, 319.
[290] Dunning, p. 192.
[291] Bailey, *Presidential Greatness*, p. 147; Smith I, pp. 583-84.

history.[292]   Before revisionism, Akerman generally was viewed as merely another questionable appointment.[293]

Grant's political alliance with Butler, a chief promoter of civil rights measures in the House of Representatives even after most politicians had given up on Reconstruction, also emerges in a different light.   Significantly, reform-oriented Hayes would assert that the "third-term talk, the Civil Rights Bill [of 1875], the partisan appointments of the baser sort, in other words the *Butlerism* of the Administration, are all bad,"[294] as if these apparently separate issues were all part of the same phenomenon.   Reconstruction provides a fuller understanding of the interconnectedness of all three matters, and it casts light on Hayes' branding of the dominant Republicans "of whom Butler is leader" as mere "corruptionists . . . ."[295]

Carl Schurz, one of Grant's principal enemies in the Senate, saw "Negro supremacy," as he viewed Reconstruction, as "the horror, the nightmare, of the Southern people," and the ramifications of Grant's seemingly despotic policy of military Reconstruction comprised a significant part of the corruption charges that historians have inherited from Grant's enemies.[296]   Woodward calls the South "the most conspicuous example of corruption" during Grant's terms,[297] and in Hesseltine's words, many Republicans during the mid-1870's came to feel that ending party corruption "involved bringing to an end the incongruous alliance between Eastern financiers and the illiterate black voters of the South . . . ."   Consequently, it "clearly meant that Grant would have to be scrapped" as well.[298]   During his 1872 campaign against Horace Greeley, "Kaiser Ulysses" had been widely denounced in both North and South for his "tyranny and despotism" while reformers equated "Grantism" with "Caesarism."[299]   Frederick Douglass, on the other hand, campaigned vigorously for the president,

---

[292]   See Barnhart.

[293]   A Georgia Confederate turned Republican, Akerman, who replaced Hoar to the chagrin of reformers, was described by his enemies as a "third-rate rebel and a fourth-rate lawyer." Hoogenboom, p. 75. See also Coolidge, p. 386.

[294]   Williams III, p. 271.

[295]   Ibid., p. 269.

[296]   Sproat, p. 11.

[297]   C.V. Woodward, p. 53.

[298]   Hesseltine, p. 372.

[299]   Current, p. 4.

asserting his sensitivity to the rights of blacks and accessibility to people regardless of race or economic status.[300]

Grant was reelected by a landslide, but it would be inaccurate to attribute his victory to Reconstruction. Most historians agree that prosperity and success in foreign affairs were more dominant electoral factors in 1872, and in fact the growing opposition to Southern intervention among Northerners would create immense difficulties during Grant's second term while the president actually sought to bring his racial agenda to new levels. At the same time, Southern whites refused to end their counterrevolution, even after the death of the Ku Klux Klan. Groups like the rifle clubs and Red Shirts of South Carolina, the White Liners of Mississippi, the White Man's Party in Alabama, and the White Leaguers of Louisiana would menace Grant during his term. These organizations sought to employ several Klan tactics and added the indirect method of intimidation by social ostracism and economic pressure.[301] On a number of occasions, Grant was called upon to respond to cases in which Southern Republican power was threatened in a particular state. One of the most misunderstood facets of Grant's Reconstruction policy, interpreting the sum of the president's individual responses, has been consistently problematic for historians.

While emphasis—and condemnation—traditionally have been placed on the instances in which Grant sent aid to Southern Republicans, Gillette, who presupposes that Grant acted to preserve the often conflictual aims of his own political fortunes, the maintenance of order, and Republican rule, is bewildered by his record: "Grant's southern policy was a study in incongruity: a curious, confusing, changeable mix of boldness and timidity, decision and indecision, activity and passivity, as he shifted between reinforcement and retrenchment, coercion and conciliation."[302] Much of this confusion stems from his study's lack of analysis of Grant's messages and papers—Gillette himself admits "the dearth of Grant manuscripts" in his research[303]—which is startling in view of the apparent comfort with which he judges the president's motives. Actually, Gillette neglects a vast wealth of evidence, some of which already has been presented, confirming Grant's enthusiasm and far-sightedness on matters of race.

---

[300] Douglass IV, p. 602.
[301] Gillette, pp. 43, 45.
[302] Ibid., pp. 166-67.
[303] Ibid., p. 439.

Perhaps research deficiencies contribute to Gillette's curious assumption of "Grant's reticence" as leading to "his noncommital, uninvolved attitude on many occasions . . . ."[304] By indiscriminately attributing every Republican fall from power in a Southern state during Reconstruction directly or indirectly to a lack of determination on Grant's part[305] (inferring an abandonment of Southern blacks), Gillette's study oversimplifies the varying factors the president faced. It certainly would not befit revisionism to label every Democratic victory in the South a defeat of the Reconstruction Amendments, for only in some instances was black Republican power strong enough to mandate victory and spur the consequential intimidation that called for federal intervention.

Grant sought to limit his use of federal troops, preferring to have problems in individual states resolved by their own state militias if possible and realizing the enormous political cost of mounting Northern opposition to what often appeared to be arbitrary intervention. Nevertheless, in a number of instances he found himself acting despite the liability involved. The frequent instability and corruption of Republican regimes, which usually were "weak and chronically unstable,"[306] sometimes complicated the matter further by presenting a no-win situation for Grant in which his intervention could serve only partisan interests at the expense of supporting flagrantly unlawful behavior.

In 1870, for example, Governor William W. Holden of North Carolina asked the president for federal troops to aid in suppressing violence during the legislative elections of that year.[307] Promising potential federal support, Grant in turn sent six companies to Raleigh to help Holden if his own state militia could not crush the violence. Federal aid did not become necessary, and Holden declared two counties—one with a small black majority, and the other with a large white majority—to be in a state of military insurrection.[308] However, the governor's expedition resulted in illegal military arrests without charge and trial and in the mistreatment of prisoners.[309] Both counties

---

[304] Ibid., p. 177.
[305] Ibid., p. 166.
[306] Ibid., p. 176.
[307] Ibid., pp. 90-91.
[308] Ibid., p. 91.
[309] Ibid., pp. 91-92.

went Republican, but Democratic success elsewhere determined the election in repudiation of the use of military force.[310] Holden, who was thereafter under the suspicion that he had attempted to manipulate the outcome of the election, was impeached and convicted in 1871 with the help of some of his own Republican allies, who regarded him as a disgrace to the party.[311]

At the same time, the president remained concerned about protecting the fruits of the Fourteenth and Fifteenth Amendments, and he was determined not to allow the intimidation of blacks to lead to the establishment of state regimes with fraudulent claims to power. His intervention in the South on several occasions, though from one standpoint motivated by constitutional considerations, seemed simultaneously to violate orthodox notions of American federalism, for Grant sometimes interfered with state governments and elections more boldly than any other president.

C. Contested Southern Elections and Presidential Intervention, 1872-1875

On four occasions between 1872 and 1875, Grant was faced with the problem of contested elections in the South, yet another dimension of the crisis he faced during Reconstruction.[312] The first such instance occurred in Louisiana, an especially problem-ridden state with a slim black majority. There, in the fall of 1872, a gubernatorial election that involved numerous illegalities on both sides ended in claims of victory by both conservative Democratic candidate John McEnery and his opponent, Republican William P. Kellogg, as well as the rest of their respective partisan teams running for the state legislature.[313] As soon as a federal circuit court issued a judgment in favor of the Republican claim, Grant, deciding that to be the better legal claim, sent federal troops and marshals to seize the statehouse. Kellogg and his legislature assumed power, and Grant ordered the federal troops to keep the government protected.[314] On December 13 and 14, the state militia

---

[310] Ibid., p. 92.
[311] Ibid., pp. 92, 94.
[312] Woolley, p. 186.
[313] Ibid., pp. 186-87; Gillette, pp. 110-11.
[314] Woolley, p. 187; Gillette, pp. 111-12.

mutinied against Kellogg, and Grant successfully ordered his forces to suppress the uprising.[315] In January 1873, McEnery and his legislature convened separately and even held inauguration ceremonies.[316] Despite Kellogg's urgings, Grant declined to have federal troops force the governor's rivals to disperse, assuring him that the troops would not allow him to be overthrown.[317]

In February, seeing that civil war probably lay ahead, Grant, in a move to consolidate his own powers in the matter, gave Congress a limited choice during the final hours of its last session: formulate a solution to Louisiana's internal problems, or he would continue to recognize Kellogg. As expected, an indecisive Congress took no action, so Grant interpreted this as approval for his course.[318] In March, the president ordered federal troops to counter an armed mob of about five hundred conservatives that was attacking a New Orleans police station, and the mob dispersed without conflict as soon as the troops arrived.[319]

The next day, Kellogg seized the McEnery faction's legislative hall, supported by unauthorized federal troops. Violence spread to the countryside and often assumed the form of race riots, the worst of which occurred at Colfax in April, when a group of blacks representing the Kellogg faction stormed a local courthouse. On April 13, they were attacked by about two hundred whites of the McEnery faction. About seventy-one blacks and two whites were killed before federal troops restored order, and the bodies of many of the blacks were found mutilated.[320] Grant considered it "a butchery of citizens . . . which in blood-thirstiness and barbarity is hardly surpassed by any acts of savage warfare."[321] Many newspapers in the North blamed the Colfax massacre not on the Louisiana whites, but on Louisiana blacks, Kellogg, and Grant for having established the regime. Early in May, the Kellogg faction, aided by the army, won another victory at St. Martinsville. On May 22, Grant ordered the McEnery faction to disperse, and the violence ended for the time being.[322]

---

[315] Gillette, p. 112.
[316] Ibid., p. 113.
[317] Ibid.; Woolley, pp. 186-88.
[318] Gillette, p. 114.
[319] Ibid., pp. 114-15.
[320] Ibid., p. 115.
[321] DuBois, p. 685.
[322] Gillette, p. 116; Hesseltine, p. 116; Woolley, p. 187.

Late in 1872 another election dispute arose in Alabama, where Democratic and Republican factions, each claiming to be the state's rightful legislatures, simultaneously convened in the state house and the federal court house respectively. Republican Governor William H. Smith, who accused the Democrats of fraud and intimidation, recognized the Republican legislature, and both sides appealed to the president for recognition.[323] On December 11, Grant submitted an unofficial plan for compromise while asking both parties in the interim to refrain from using "military or other force . . . ."[324] Facing federal troops in Montgomery, the Democrats meanwhile were forced to halt their opposition as the Republicans managed to secure control of both houses of the legislature.[325]

In December 1873, a Democratic governor and legislature were elected in Texas by a landslide, and the head of the incumbent Republican government, Governor Edmund J. Davis, attempted to extend his party's rule through a state supreme court judgment declaring the election illegal and void.[326] His claim contained little validity, but in January 1874, Davis threatened to sustain his government with the president's aid.[327] Grant refused to intervene, however, and reminded the Texas Republicans that they had in fact passed their state's election laws and willingly campaigned under them, not to protest until after they lost: "Would it not be prudent, as well as right, to yield to the verdict of the people as expressed by their ballots?"[328] As many historians have failed to understand, Grant's policy of intervention in the South was neither shrilly partisan nor incoherent and confusing. Texas, a fairly typical example of the Democratic tendencies of a predominantly white state, illustrates Grant's refusal to allow party loyalty to impede the proper execution of the law.

The example of Arkansas marks how a shift in the black Republican power base greatly complicated the situation Grant faced. In 1874, civil war in that state presented the president with a new crisis. The unrest originated in the controversial gubernatorial election of 1872

---

[323] Woolley, p. 188; Gillette, p. 95.
[324] Woolley, p. 188.
[325] Woolley, pp. 188-89; Gillette, pp. 97-98.
[326] Woolley, p. 189; Gillette, p. 101.
[327] Woolley, pp. 189-90.
[328] Ibid., p. 190. See also Gillette, pp. 101-02.

between regular (pro-Grant) Republican Elisha Baxter and Liberal Republican Joseph Brooks, who was allied with the state's Democrats.[329]   Baxter represented the Republican organization of incumbent Governor Powell Clayton, the fragile power of which relied upon the black vote and the disfranchisement of about 20,000 former Confederates.[330] Both Baxter and Brooks claimed to have been elected, but since the state legislature declared Baxter the governor (largely through the fraudulent intervention of politicos), he was initially installed.[331]   Brooks irregularly obtained from a lower state circuit judge an order ousting Baxter, and he successfully seized control of state buildings on April 15, 1874.[332]   Both appealed to Grant for recognition, but the president initially ordered only that federal forces in Little Rock prevent violence between the two factions, which had the effect of preserving the *status quo* and allowing Brooks to remain.[333] Random mob violence developed in several parts of the state, and Grant finally broke his neutrality and recognized Baxter on May 15 on the advice of Attorney General Williams, who claimed that the legislature's support made him the rightful governor.[334]   The Brooks faction was ordered to disperse, and they surrendered the statehouse on May 19.[335]

Baxter, however, had surprised and alienated the Clayton faction by accommodating Democrats while Brooks gravitated toward the regular Republicans.[336]   In July, a state constitutional convention, ordered by the Democratic legislature and warmly approved by Baxter, framed a new constitution that restored suffrage to disfranchised whites and stipulated that the incumbent governor's term would expire that November.[337]   Meanwhile, Brooks, who had made as sharp a political turn as Baxter, asserted the illegality of the new constitution with the new support of black Republicans.[338]   Refusing to recognize the new

---

[329]   Woolley, p. 190; Gillette, p. 137; DuBois, pp. 551-52.

[330]   DuBois, pp. 551-52.

[331]   Woolley, pp. 190-91; Gillette, p. 137.   Historians generally agree that Brooks was legally elected in 1872.

[332]   Woolley, p. 191; Gillette, p. 138.

[333]   Woolley, p. 191; Gillette, p. 139.

[334]   Woolley, p. 191; Richardson IX, pp. 4226-27; DuBois, p. 552; Gillette, pp. 138-43.

[335]   Woolley, p. 191; Gillette, p. 143; DuBois, p. 552.

[336]   Woolley, p. 192; Gillette, pp. 137-38.

[337]   Woolley, pp. 191-92; Gillette, p. 144.

[338]   Woolley, p. 192.

constitution, Republicans did not choose a candidate for the October 13 gubernatorial election, and Democrat Augustus H. Garland was easily elected.[339]

While exploring the matter, Grant decided that allowing the new constitution to stand would be a dangerous precedent undermining Reconstruction, and he determined that intervention was necessary, as in the case of Louisiana.[340] However, this entailed a dramatic about-face from his previous stand: both Garland and Baxter would be repudiated while Brooks, the legally elected governor in 1872, would be restored to power under the original constitution (according to which Brooks' term would not expire until 1877). At the same time, Congress was conducting an on-the-spot investigation that was expected to result in a resolution supporting federal intervention. Grant's recommendation to Congress seemed more like a command, for he threatened to depose Garland and install Brooks himself and seemed only to be seeking an excuse for such action.[341] Northern opposition to intervention was almost universal, and many newspapers condemned Grant's Southern policy as a failure.[342]

On March 2, 1875, the lame-duck Republican House of Representatives decisively defeated the motion to recognize Brooks and passed the Poland resolution, which recognized both Garland and the new constitution.[343] This resolution, a far cry from the congressional response to Louisiana, upset Grant's plans for Arkansas, although his assertiveness was a clear warning to other Southern states not to follow Arkansas' example and made a desperate Garland promise to punish all terrorist offenders in his state.[344] Still, the striking political irregularities in Arkansas' already fragile condition made Grant's only workable alternative to abandonment an awkward (if not impossible) one: he was attempting to restore a regime that was dead for almost a year thanks to his own efforts.[345] A supportive public might have dealt more sympathetically with the complexities of the matter, but the apparent lack of credibility of both claimants of the governorship and

---

[339] Ibid.; DuBois, p. 552.
[340] Gillette, pp. 145-46.
[341] Ibid., p. 147.
[342] Ibid., pp. 147-48.
[343] Ibid., pp. 146, 148.
[344] Ibid., pp. 149, 146.
[345] Ibid., pp. 149-50.

the onus of tyranny could hope to find little support in the midst of growing hostility.

The Kellogg government's dependence upon federal support for its very existence was demonstrated in 1874. On September 14 and 15, the McEnery forces, aided by White Leaguers, mounted a successful *coup d'etat* in New Orleans.[346]   Ordering the rebels to disperse and dispatching five thousand troops and three gunboats to New Orleans, Grant successfully crushed the insurgency by the 17th.[347] Another crisis arose on November 2, when Democrats used open intimidation and covert fraud during the election for the state legislature.[348] Anticipating problems when the legislature gathered in January, Grant authorized General Philip H. Sheridan on December 24 to investigate the matter and to assume command if necessary; he also explored the possibility of placing Louisiana under martial law.[349]   Surely enough, crisis came on January 4, 1875, when anti-Kellogg forces illegally entered the lower chamber and attempted to gain control by seating five Democrats.[350]

What followed was the most controversial instance of federal intervention in the South.   Sheridan proceeded to eject the five Democrats from the statehouse, restoring Republican control, and the nation was swept with anger toward Washington, fueled further by Sheridan's suggestion that White Leaguers be treated as "banditti" and shot as outlaws.[351]   (In fact, the first fifteen days of January saw the adoption of more states' rights resolutions than the preceding fifteen years.[352]) Many Republicans, including Vice-President Henry Wilson, lamented the devastating political blow of Grant's actions.[353]   Grant refused to join the condemnation of Sheridan, but he did successfully end national outbursts in his January 13 message to the Senate; he also aroused negative feelings toward Louisiana Democrats.[354] Explaining his actions in terms of his responsibility to enforce the Fifteenth

---

[346] Ibid., p. 118.
[347] Ibid., pp. 119-20.
[348] Ibid., p. 121.
[349] Ibid., p. 122.
[350] Ibid., p. 123.
[351] Current, p. 4; McFeely, p. 417; Gillette, p. 124.
[352] Gillette, p. 124.
[353] Ibid., p. 125.
[354] Ibid., pp. 128-30.

Amendment—a duty that was "too clear for controversy"—he condemned the racial and political injustice in Louisiana:

> To hold the people of Louisiana generally responsible for these atrocities would not be just, but it is a lamentable fact that insuperable obstructions were thrown in the way of punishing these murderers; and the so-called conservative papers of the State not only justified the massacre, but denounced as Federal tyranny and despotism the attempt . . . to bring them to justice. Fierce denunciations ring through the country about office holding and election matters in Louisiana, while every one of the Colfax miscreants goes unwhipped of justice, and no way can be found in this boasted land of civilization and Christianity to punish the perpetrators of this bloody and monstrous crime. . . . [Last August, some] Northern young men . . . . [in Coushatta, Louisiana,] were Republicans and officeholders under Kellogg. They were therefore doomed to death. . . . No one has been punished, and the conservative press of the State denounced all efforts to that end and boldly justified the crime. . . .
>
> To say that the murder of a negro or a white Republican is not considered a crime in Louisiana would probably be unjust to a great part of the people, but . . . a great number of such murders have been committed and no one has been punished therefor; and manifestly, as to them, the spirit of hatred and violence is stronger than law.[355]

In March, the Senate approved Grant's actions and recognized Kellogg as the lawful governor.[356] Democratic agreement not to dispute Kellogg's status as governor came with the Wheeler Compromise of April 17, which also decided that the state's lower house would be Democratic while the state senate would remain Republican.[357] Gillette criticizes Grant's recognition of Kellogg in the first place as "a serious miscalculation," noting that Louisiana's burden "simply dragged down" the Republican Party.[358] The president, alleged by his critic to have been driven "by both political considerations and cronyism,"[359] certainly did not benefit politically from Louisiana, but Grant's real achievement eludes Gillette: aware of public opposition, yet maintaining the initiative, Grant secured the fruits of political equality

---

[355] Richardson IX, pp. 4262-63.

[356] Gillette, p. 131.

[357] Ibid., p. 132.

[358] Ibid., p. 134.

[359] Ibid., p. 133.

in a predominantly black state by taking action that, despite its ultimate limited success in the state legislature, probably saved Kellogg's regime from being deposed.

D. Grappling with Reconstruction amid Escalating Opposition during Grant's Second Term

It is interesting to note how much more readily pre-revisionist historians assert Grant's dedication to Reconstruction during a historiographical period that sees it as misguided. While the Dunning school widely criticized Grant for refusing to abandon his original objectives for Southern blacks, post-revisionists in Gillette's school actually point to Grant as a culprit in the retreat from Reconstruction, especially during his second term. (Examples already have been provided that refute this school of thought.) Gillette and McFeely fail to take into account the full political and legal context in which Grant was working. Federal intervention on occasions other than insurrection was politically and legally best applied as a last resort when it was clear that state authorities could not handle a particular situation. Northern opposition was extensive enough by 1874 to increase Grant's legal scruples by necessity. In fact, this opposition contributed to the Republican electoral defeats in 1874, which gave the House of Representatives to their rivals. The Democratic House between 1875 and 1877 deprived the president of a valuable tool for advancing his legislative civil rights agenda.

In four somewhat ambiguous cases between 1874 and 1875, cases that did not involve disputed elections, Grant responded to calls for troops with caution, deciding in two cases that sufficient troops were already available to suppress violence. On July 29, 1874, Republican Governor Adelbert Ames of Mississippi requested federal troops to help suppress the impending conflict in the Vicksburg area, where armed Republicans and Democrats stood ready to battle during the city's elections in August.[360] Grant refused the requested troops for lack of jurisdiction, but this was hardly a decision of timidity. The violence was confined to a municipal level, and it was not applying unrealistic logic to assume that the ideal of nonintervention could be maintained while the state could handle such a situation itself,

---

[360] Woolley, p. 194.

especially in view of the fact that Ames had made his call without attempting to utilize his own forces and months before declaring a state of insurrection.[361]   Grant also showed reasonable restraint on September 25, when he responded to South Carolina Governor Franklin J. Moses' call for troops to counter armed bands in Edgefield County: the company of federal troops already in the county, he pointed out, would be sufficient protection.[362]

The Democrats in the vicinity of Vicksburg meanwhile were mounting a campaign of racial intimidation during which about three hundred blacks and two whites were killed on or after December 7, 1874.   In response to this crisis, Ames finally declared a state of insurrection and convened the state legislature, which proceeded to call upon Grant for aid.[363]   Grant ordered the "disorderly and turbulent persons" to disperse on December 21, and when federal troops arrived in January, they proceeded to seize the Warren County (Vicksburg) courthouse and to replace the fraudulently installed Democratic sheriff with a Republican.[364]

Throughout Grant's presidency, the sole instance in which the failure to supply troops upon request allowed a subsequent revolution of intimidation to immerse a legitimate regime came in Mississippi in 1875.   Grant, McFeely contends in typical contemptuous form, "was not ready to use his authority or his troops to persuade white Mississippi that the federal government would refuse to acquiesce to the demise of black rights or to racial massacres."[365]   This episode in Mississippi, an exception, tends to be magnified by Grant's post-revisionist debunkers as reflective of a rule—namely, Grant's indifference—which is further problematic when one considers the lack of analysis behind such assertions as McFeely's.   On September 8, 1875, four days after the massacre of about thirty-four blacks at Clinton, Ames requested federal assistance in suppressing violence, citing disorder in three counties.   At this point, opposition to federal intervention was "widespread" in the North and "desperate" in the South.[366]

---

[361] Gillette, pp. 150-52; Woolley, p. 194.
[362] Woolley, pp. 194-95.
[363] Gillette, p. 151.
[364] Ibid.; Woolley, p. 195.
[365] McFeely, p. 422.
[366] Woolley, p. 195; Gillette, p. 155.

Many Republicans tried to convince Grant that if he intervened in Mississippi, the critical Ohio gubernatorial election would be lost. Barraged with varying reports of the violence, including a flood of contradictions to Ames' characterization of the situation, what would Grant decide? On September 13, Attorney General Pierrepont, who had replaced Williams in May, received a response from Grant: the "whole public are tired out with these annual, autumnal outbreaks in the South, and there is so much unwholesome lying done by the press and people in regard to the cause and extent of these breaches of the peace that the great majority are ready now to condemn any interference on the part of the Government."[367] This passage is often quoted alone in accounts of the situation, but the remainder of the letter is vital in understanding Grant's decision: "I heartily wish that peace and good order may be restored without issuing the proclamation [to disperse]. But if it is not, the proclamation must be issued; and if it is, I shall instruct the commander of the forces to have no child's play."[368]

Grant's "refusal" to send troops, as many accounts represent it, was actually not a refusal at all, but an assurance. In fact, the president initially had ordered troops to prepare to receive orders to suppress any uncontrollable insurrection,[369] and he remarked, "I do not see how we are to evade the call of the Governor, if made strictly within the Constitution and Acts of Congress."[370] However, Pierrepont, a strict constructionist, used his role as intermediary to narrow in effect Grant's interpretation of the scope of federal authority. He conveyed the wrong impression to others by quoting the president out of context, and he misrepresented the severity of the situation to Grant by ignoring the relationship between violence and fraudulent Democratic electoral victory.[371]

Ames further muddled the situation by striking a naive "treaty of peace" with his opponents: he promised to demobilize and disarm two

---

[367] Gillette, p. 157.
[368] Woolley, pp. 196-97. Gillette and McFeely quote from the first part of Grant's message without including these key sentences. See Gillette, p. 157; McFeely, p. 422. Gillette alters the context for his readers by quoting the words "no child's play" only at the close of his chapter on Mississippi, for purposes of criticism. Gillette, p. 164.
[369] Gillette, p. 156.
[370] Ibid., p. 157.
[371] Ibid., pp. 157-58.

militia companies while organizing no new ones, and the Democrats pledged to terminate their terrorist campaign, a promise of limited trustworthiness that would be followed by an eerie period of relative calm among the races.[372] Ames also hurt the likelihood that federal troops would come to his aid by giving the impression that the problem had been solved. He wrote to Grant in late September, "Your letter and Atty. General Pierrepont's have produced marked improvement in the condition of affairs here. The white liners, whose only policy is intimidation, are themselves somewhat intimidated."[373] He continued to call for troops but evaded specific questions about the urgency of the situation. (At the last moment, some troops were authorized from Washington only to suppress disorder, not to police polling places.)[374] The weight of the evidence Grant saw clearly favored nonintervention.[375]

Election Day passed with primarily silent intimidation (little violence actually being involved), but significant losses in Republican strength in about 21 of 72 counties in the state, combined with the increased turnout of whites, was enough for the Democrats to win the state legislature.[376]   In March 1876, Ames faced the start of impeachment proceedings by the new, intensely hostile legislature, and he resigned under this pressure, a move that returned his state to Democratic rule.[377]

Grant would declare that the new Mississippi government was comprised of "officials chosen through fraud and violence such as would scarcely be accredited to savages, much less to a civilized and Christian people."[378] Although this was a defeat for Southern blacks— and thus for Grant's policy—the facts of the case do not legitimize the conclusion that this marked a presidential abandonment of Black Americans. The episode was marked by various miscommunications between Ames, Pierrepont, and Grant, and by Ames' failure to provide important information about the urgency of the situation.[379] Grant later

---

[372] Harris, pp. 672-73; Gillette, p. 161.
[373] Gillette, p. 161.
[374] Ibid., pp. 156, 161-62.
[375] Harris, p. 666.
[376] Ibid., pp. 684-87.
[377] Ibid., pp. 697-98.
[378] Hesseltine, p. 409.
[379] See generally Gillette, pp. 155-65.

told Congressman John R. Lynch that he had prepared orders to assist Ames but ultimately decided with great reluctance that while his intervention would not have affected the outcome of the Mississippi election, it would decisively incur Republican defeat in Ohio's October 1875 election—an agonizing decision Grant later said would not have been made had he thought he could save Mississippi.[380]

It may reasonably be asked to what extent Grant's Southern policy looked beyond party considerations to the enforcement of the Fourteenth and Fifteenth Amendments, but the record of increasing opposition to Reconstruction during the 1870's indicates that Grant actually compromised his own political health for the sake of realizing what he saw as the broader meaning of Union victory. It is true that his intervention in the South, when it did occur, invariably aided the Republicans, but in doing so, Grant also bolstered the black political power base that often had a suppressed but substantial enough claim to determine state electoral outcomes (to the violent disgust of many Southern whites). In the 1870's, there appeared at times to be a fine line between dedication to the Fourteenth and Fifteenth Amendments and Republican partisanship.[381]

From the outset, Grant displayed an awareness of the "prejudice to color" as the root of the problem that faced him. This prejudice would be manifested as an ongoing, intense opposition to black political power, a factor so pervasive and a cause so fundamental to the persistent white counterrevolution that Grant ultimately was faced with a choice between disloyalty to the Black American and political injury. (Had a less popular president been in Grant's place, the latter choice might have been outright political destruction.) The Democratic Party, which served as a political channel for anti-black sentiment, naturally would prevail in Southern states with white majorities as long as the Republicans remained faithful to a racial agenda. Continued Northern support for Reconstruction might have made a difference, but it is a fundamental consideration that the "prejudice to color," though not nearly as violent, permeated that section of the country as well. Garfield had noted that Northern enthusiasm for Reconstruction was a short-term response to victory in war that soon would subside due to the "general apathy among the people" toward blacks.[382] The extraordinary

---

[380] Lynch, pp. 150-53. See also Harris, p. 668.
[381] See Gillette, pp. 46-47.
[382] Ibid., p. 131.

exertion of federal muscle to assist Southern blacks was condemned by a population that was concerned more with impending economic matters.

Catton paraphrases the nation's emerging view of Reconstruction as follows: "For Heaven's sake, sweep the whole mess under the rug if you can't do anything else, but at least get it out of sight so we can go on about our ordinary business!"[383] When blacks failed to assert their rights, they were dismissed as backward beyond redemption. When they attempted to protect their power, they were derided as obnoxious demagogues.[384] Whatever laws existed, deeply embedded social attitudes precluded a lasting consensus in favor of Reconstruction.[385] In the midst of these mounting impediments to Reconstruction, however, Grant, working in a direction that ran counter to popular sentiment, brought his racial agenda to a new level.

In his Second Inaugural Address in 1873, Grant expanded the request he had made four years earlier, indicating that Black Americans were entitled to more than the ballot:

> The effects of the late civil strife have been to free the slave and make him a citizen. Yet he is not possessed of the civil rights which citizenship should carry with it. This is wrong, and should be corrected. To this correction I stand committed, so far as Executive influence can avail.
>
> Social equality is not a subject to be legislated upon, nor shall I ask that anything be done to advance the social status of the colored man, except to give him a fair chance to develop what there is good in him, give him access to the schools, and when he travels let him feel assured that his conduct will regulate the treatment and fare he will receive.[386]

In his Fifth Annual Message in December 1873, the president repeated his request for "a law to better secure the civil rights which freedom should secure, but has not effectually secured, to the enfranchised slave."[387]

---

383 Catton, p. 180.
384 Gillette, p. 196.
385 Ibid., p. 196.
386 Richardson IX, p. 4175.
387 Ibid., p. 4209.

After the electoral defeats of 1874, lame-duck Republicans in the House passed the Civil Rights Act in 1875, which Grant signed on March 1. (House Republicans failed to secure passage of a proposed enforcement bill, dubbed by some of its enemies as "Grant's bayonet bill," which would have expanded existing federal election enforcement laws.[388] As it turned out, even if it had passed, much of it probably would have become a dead letter under the Supreme Court's narrow interpretation of the Fourteenth and Fifteenth Amendments the following year.) The Civil Rights Act prohibited racial discrimination in public transportation and accommodations of many kinds, as well as in jury selection, and it evoked enormous opposition from the many political leaders who were determined to be done with Radical Reconstruction. "To many liberals," writes Sproat, "the Supplementary Civil Rights Act of 1875 was almost as deplorable as the scandals."[389] Republicans worried that such a measure would hurt the party, and indeed it cost Grant considerable support from border state Republicans.[390]

Additionally, DuBois points out, many blacks "sank into apathy and fatalism," which illustrates another impediment to Grant's Reconstruction policies: the lack of initiative and resolve among blacks sufficient to stop the Southern counterrevolution.[391] While the civil rights legislation nine decades later would be initiated by a determined large-scale movement among blacks who had substantially defined their rights before bringing their case to the government, it was the government that paved the road to political and civil equality during Reconstruction, often with the newly freed slaves trailing behind with less momentum than time allowed them to develop. Nevertheless, Gillette's ironically Dunning-like criticism of the act as "meaningless"[392] and as a mere "catalyst that greatly hastened the reaction against reconstruction" places the blame on Republicans themselves "for giving such ammunition to their opponents."[393] Although blacks utilized the law on a relatively sparse basis and the

---

[388] Gillette, pp. 284, 291.
[389] Sproat, p. 89.
[390] Hesseltine, p. 357.
[391] DuBois, pp. 701-02.
[392] Gillette, p. 273.
[393] Ibid., p. 258.

Supreme Court would invalidate it in the *Civil Rights Cases*[394] in 1883, Gillette's assessment is inaccurate. Many attempts at integration in public places did succeed, and as Foner asserts, the law was "a broad assertion of principle" that "represented an unprecedented exercise of national authority . . . ."[395]

Drawing even more criticism than the Civil Rights Act was Grant's military intervention in the South. The president's use of troops in Louisiana in 1875 evoked mass meetings in the North as well as bitter condemnation from members of Congress, and liberal and moderate Republicans grew increasingly worried that Grant's Reconstruction policies were hurting the party.[396] Even Vice-President Wilson, who in his legislative career had established an impeccable record in support of Reconstruction as a Radical, told Garfield that Grant was "the mill-stone around the neck of our party that would sink it out of sight." Garfield himself declared in his diary on the day he learned about the event in Louisiana, "This is on the whole the darkest day for the Republican Party and its hopes I have ever seen since the war."[397] It was figures outside the mainstream, such as Frederick Douglass and Wendell Phillips, who praised Grant's actions in Louisiana, and this praise did not compare to the storm of condemnation.[398]

Even before he intervened in Louisiana, Grant fully recognized the unpopularity of federal interference in the South, and he addressed the issue in his Sixth Annual Message in 1874, beginning with a lament over the events that had taken place in several Southern states:

> I regret to say that with preparations for the late election decided indications appeared in some localities in the Southern States of a determination, by acts of violence and intimidation, to deprive citizens of the freedom of the ballot because of their political opinions. Bands of men, masked and armed, made their appearance; White Leagues and other societies were formed; large quantities of arms and ammunition were imported and distributed to these organizations; military drills, with menacing demonstrations, were held, and with all these murders enough were committed to spread terror among those whose political action was to be suppressed, if possible, by these intolerant and criminal

---

[394] 109 U.S. 3.
[395] Foner, p. 556.
[396] Hesseltine, pp. 349-50.
[397] Garfield III, p. 6.
[398] Douglass IV, pp. 404-05; Hesseltine, p. 355.

proceedings. In some places colored laborers were compelled to vote according to the wishes of their employers, under threats of discharge if they acted otherwise; and there are too many instances in which, when these threats were disregarded, they were remorselessly executed by those who made them. I understand that the fifteenth amendment to the Constitution was made to prevent this and a like state of things, and the [Enforcement] act of May 31, 1870, with amendments, was passed to enforce its provisions, the object of both being to guarantee to all citizens the right to vote and to protect them in the free enjoyment of that right. Enjoined by the Constitution "to take care that the laws be faithfully executed," and convinced by undoubted evidence that violations of said act had been committed and that a widespread and flagrant disregard of it was contemplated, the proper officers were instructed to prosecute the offenders, and troops were stationed at convenient points to aid these officers, if necessary, in the performance of their official duties. Complaints are made of this interference by Federal authority; but if said amendment and act do not provide for such interference under the circumstances as above stated, then they are without meaning, force, or effect, and *the whole scheme of colored enfranchisement is worse than mockery and little better than a crime.* [emphasis added][399]

Acknowledging that his interference "with the affairs of a State" was "repugnant to public opinion," the president conveyed his desire to avoid such actions and asserted their legitimacy when he took them, aiming the blame at the failure of white Southerners to respect the rights of their black neighbors:

I desire . . . that all necessity for Executive direction in local affairs may become unnecessary and obsolete. I invite the attention . . . of the people . . . to the causes and effects of these unhappy questions. . . . I believe . . . the better part of . . . [the Southern people have] a disposition to be law abiding . . . . But do they do right in ignoring the existence of violence and bloodshed in resistance to constituted authority? I sympathize with their prostrate condition . . . . But can they proclaim themselves entirely irresponsible for this condition? They can not. . . . [Rampant violence in some localities] has either been justified or denied by those who could have prevented it. The theory . . . that there is to be no further interference on the part of the General Government to protect citizens within a State where the State authorities fail to give protection. . . . is a great mistake. While I

---

[399] Richardson IX, p. 4251.

remain Executive all the laws of Congress and the provisions of the Constitution . . . will be enforced with rigor, but with regret that they should have added one jot or tittle to Executive duties or powers. Let there be fairness in the discussion of Southern questions . . . condemning the wrong and upholding the right, and soon all will be well. . . . *Treat the negro as a citizen and a voter, as he is and must remain . . . . Then we shall have no complaint of sectional interference.* [emphasis added][400]

Despite such pleas, the capacity for Northerners to "be perturbed over the persecution of carpetbaggers by the 'men of property and intelligence' in the South" clearly was diminishing.[401]   As Carpenter asserts,

More clearly than many other Northern Republicans, Grant sensed what was happening in the South. His efforts to stem the tide brought him little but denunciation from those who could only see what damage was being done to the party, or who preferred orderly white-controlled government in the Southern states to seemingly unrepresentative, sometimes corrupt, and frequently inept carpetbag regimes.   That the Negro would be stripped of most of what gains he had achieved during Reconstruction was merely seen as a price that had to be paid.[402]

Gillette errs in confining Grant's strategy to realizing "momentary objectives—political or personal."[403]   By defining and pursuing goals that "could hardly have been accomplished within one generation" [404]— but that nevertheless comprised the realization of the Fourteenth and Fifteenth Amendments—Grant defied the "momentary" constraints of his time in order to perpetuate a civil order of American equality in accordance with the government's blueprint. Far from being a culprit in the retreat from Reconstruction, as Gillette and McFeely infer, Grant remained dedicated to the rights of Black Americans after most Republicans had abandoned the cause.

The president's failure to embrace popular sentiment on Reconstruction marks one dimension of his administration that did show

---

[400] Ibid., pp. 4252-53.
[401] Hesseltine, p. 399.
[402] Carpenter, p. 145.
[403] Gillette, p. 185.
[404] Ibid., p. 365.

signs of enervation. Woodward calls Reconstruction a "great drain" on Grant's popularity.[405] As Radicals became the dwindling minority in the country, a trend signified by Republican losses in the election of 1874, it is understandable that the Stalwart "cabal" that surrounded Grant seemed more and more like a negative influence. That the drain of Reconstruction on Grant's popularity was not greater than it was— that he basically remained a popular president—attests to his ability to maintain respect by his conduct in other realms (as well as the endurance of his Civil War-era prestige). On matters of Reconstruction, however, Grant was, in a sense, a "lame-duck" during his last two years in office: he could pursue his own policy until 1877, but his successor was likely to adopt the popular course of nonintervention. Another essential actor in Reconstruction, the Supreme Court, bolstered this "lame-duck" status besides crippling existing policies in *Reese* and *Cruikshank*.

It is understandable why the Radical members of Grant's "cabal" would have thought a third term necessary to the perpetuation of Reconstruction.[406] As Catton phrased it, "The extremists wanted to nominate Grant for a third term, but it just could not be done."[407] It was difficult, if not impossible, to find someone else with both comparable prestige and as strong an accompanying trait of firmness to carry out such an unpopular policy. Frederick Douglass had praised Grant in 1872 as "a good man, a true man, a steady man. . . . for he does not turn with every wind of doctrine,"[408] but in 1875, the upcoming presidential contest triggered his anxiety about Black Americans: "OUR SHELTER in the storms of the past has been Ulysses S. Grant. The question is as to who will shield us in the future."[409] As it turned out, Republican leaders, recognizing the wide identification of the president with Reconstruction, made considerable efforts to distance Grant from Hayes during the 1876 campaign.[410]

Refuting McFeely's contention on Grant's racial apathy, Simpson asserts, "It is not true . . . that by 'the summer of 1876 there was no one

---

[405] C.V. Woodward, p. 56.

[406] Douglass IV, p. 322.

[407] Catton, p. 180. Of course, historians have seen no problem in expecting Grant to venture far beyond the mainstream in his pursuit of the civil service reformers' agenda.

[408] Douglass IV, p. 322.

[409] Ibid., p. 418.

[410] Gillette, p. 365; Benedict, p. 374.

around the White House who gave a damn about the black people,' since the principal occupant of that building obviously did."[411] As the nation approached its centennial, Grant suggested in his Seventh Annual Message that a constitutional amendment be adopted establishing in each state a system of free public schools "irrespective of sex, color, birthplace, or religions . . . ."[412] In 1876, South Carolina and Louisiana, two of the three states with black majorities, held gubernatorial elections, and threats of violence prompted Grant to utilize troops to prevent fraud in those states. In July 1876, Republican Governor Daniel H. Chamberlain of South Carolina appealed to Grant for support, citing race riots that were mounting to intimidate blacks in the fall election.[413] Grant responded that the violence was "cruel, blood-thirsty, wanton, unprovoked and uncalled for," but that it was "only a repetition of the course that has been pursued in other Southern States in the past few years. . . . I'll give every aid for which I can find law or constitutional power."[414]

As election day approached, rifle clubs escalated their open intimidation, and Grant issued a proclamation on October 17 ordering them to disperse; he also sent troops to keep the elections untainted by fraud, though the state's votes were ultimately in dispute.[415] On October 31, Grant ordered Sheridan to protect the state returning board in Louisiana, a body that was charged with fraud prevention.[416] Republican Stephen B. Packard was facing Francis T. Nicholls in the Louisiana gubernatorial election while in South Carolina, Chamberlain was being challenged by Wade Hampton. The factions of Nicholls and Hampton, both of whom were former Confederates, hoped to secure victory by intimidation.[417] Limited in the number of troops at his disposal during the election, Grant later remarked that he would have been justified in using the army in several states "if there had been more military force available."[418] The elections ended in dispute.[419]

---

[411] Simpson, "Butcher?," p. 82.
[412] Richardson IX, p. 4288.
[413] Gillette, pp. 315-17.
[414] Hesseltine, p. 409.
[415] Ibid., p. 410; Gillette, p. 318.
[416] Gillette, p. 315.
[417] Ibid., pp. 314-16.
[418] Current, p. 5.
[419] Hesseltine, pp. 410, 414.

The consequent presidential electoral crisis absorbed both South Carolina and Louisiana, and the Compromise of 1877 gave the presidency to Hayes with the understanding that he would end federal intervention in the South.[420] In his Eighth Annual Message, Grant delivered his last address to Congress, defending his Southern policy with a brief definition of the question of Reconstruction as

> whether the control of the Government should be thrown immediately into the hands of those who had so recently and persistently tried to destroy it, or whether the victors should continue to have an equal voice with them in this control. Reconstruction, as finally agreed upon, means this and only this, except that the late slave was enfranchised, giving an increase, as was supposed, to the Union-loving and Union-supporting votes. If *free* in the full sense of the word, they would not disappoint this expectation. [emphasis in original][421]

In January, Chamberlain and Packard were inaugurated with great Democratic opposition. Grant fully supported Chamberlain, who polled the largest Republican majority in South Carolina history,[422] but he only tentatively supported Packard in Louisiana until his victory was confirmed.[423] Hayes was publicly inaugurated on March 5, and in April, the new president withdrew the last remaining troops from South Carolina and Louisiana.[424] The Republican regimes in those states, which had retained power only because of the support of federal troops,[425] soon succumbed to Democratic rule, and Reconstruction was officially over as the Solid South was born.[426]

Grant, whose policy stood repudiated, remarked, "If I had been in Mr. Hayes's place, I would have insisted upon the Republican Governor [Packard] being seated, or I would have refused to accept the

---

[420] Ibid., p. 421.
[421] Richardson IX, p. 4354.
[422] Foner, p. 575.
[423] Hesseltine, p. 421.
[424] Ibid., p. 582; Gillette, pp. 344-45. The "withdrawal" did not involve an entire physical withdrawal from the states, as is commonly assumed, but the troops' return to their barracks from their stations. Foner, p. 582.
[425] Current, p. 5.
[426] Richardson IX, p. 4288; Foner, p. 582; Hesseltine, p. 421; Gillette, pp. 344-45.

electoral vote of Louisiana."[427] When the great railroad strike broke out in July 1877, Hayes sent federal troops to suppress the strikers. Grant commented in August,

> During my two terms of office the whole Democratic press, and the morbidly honest and "reformatory" portion of the Republican press, thought it horrible to keep U.S. troops stationed in the Southern States, and when they were called upon to protect the lives of negroes—as much citizens under the Constitution as if their skins were white—the country was scarcely large enough to hold the sound of indignation belched forth by them for some years. Now, however, there is no hesitation about exhausting the whole power of the government to suppress a strike on the slightest intimation that danger threatens.[428]

Grant later lamented that "no one can look on satisfied and see" black citizens deprived of the ballot.[429] In his *Personal Memoirs*, he predicted future conflict over the status of Black Americans: "It is possible that the question of a conflict between races may come up in the future, as did that between freedom and slavery before. The condition of the colored man within our borders may become a source of anxiety, to say the least."[430] Whatever could be said about the race problem, it was "our duty to inflict no further wrong upon the negro."[431]

E. Understanding a Presidency; Sorting through a Historiographical Quagmire

Along with a refutation of the Dunning school and a realization of the primary role Grant played during the last eight years of Reconstruction comes a reconsideration of fundamental ideas about President Grant that historians have tended to embrace. The notion that Grant was a president of little substance—that he was "a hapless puppet for the Congressional Radicals," that he "was without policies" and "displayed a total lack of vision"[432]—must be viewed as the product of

---

[427] Hesseltine, p. 425.
[428] Gillette, p. 348.
[429] Young, *Around the World* II, p. 361.
[430] Grant, *Personal Memoirs* II, p. 550.
[431] Library of Congress.
[432] Tugwell, p. 223; Nevins, p. 811.

thinking that is based in contempt for the course the president pursued. Hesseltine tries to illustrate Grant's "preference for practical politicians over theorists" and how the president's "sense of the practical exceeded his appreciation of esoteric ethics," and he leaves little room for his readers to consider that the sometimes impractical course Grant followed with regard to the South could have resulted from ideals rather than from the partisan influence of unsavory allies.[433] While it is easy to attribute Grant's inaugural assertion that he had no policy "to enforce against the will of the people" to an inept confusion of the will of the people with the law of the land, Grant ironically found himself reverting to actions in defense of the Fourteenth and Fifteenth Amendments on a scale that would be unsurpassed by his successors in the face of the almost consensual opposition of the people.[434]

Contrary to the notion of President Grant as a man of no policy whose leadership was ultimately superficial, no presidential transition in American history has equaled Grant's exit in 1877, which truly marked the end of Reconstruction, as a decisive national shift on a major issue of American democracy.[435] "The negro," *The Nation* announced upon Hayes' withdrawal of federal troops, "will disappear from the field of national politics. Henceforth, the nation, as a nation, will have nothing more to do with him."[436] As Foner writes, 1877 "marked a definitive turning point in American history"—"a decisive retreat from the idea, born during the Civil War, of a powerful national state protecting the fundamental rights of American citizens."[437]

Grant's administration effected a remarkable culmination of egalitarian breakthroughs after the Civil War, and his adherence to the principles embodied in the Fourteenth and Fifteenth Amendments led to some of the boldest peacetime assertions of federal authority in American history. Federal troops are, as a rule, imperfect instruments for securing long-term constitutional goals, but in Grant's case, they were necessary as the only means to command obedience in the face of extraordinary white Southern recalcitrance against black political power.[438] (Grant also was limited by the unavailability of troops. The

---

[433] Hesseltine, p. 254.
[434] Richardson VIII, p. 3960.
[435] Franklin, p. 288.
[436] "The Political South Hereafter," *The Nation*, Apr. 5, 1877, p. 202.
[437] Foner, pp. xxvii, 582.
[438] Gillette, pp. 171, 173-74.

number of federal troops in the South in 1869, while three states were under military rule, was 11,000; at the end of 1876, there were 6,000 deployed in several small garrisons. As has been seen, while Grant was forced to limit his use of troops during the election of 1876, he later remarked that he would have been justified in using the army in several states "if there had been more military force available."[439]) While Reconstruction historians persist in confining their focus to presidential and congressional Reconstruction during Johnson's term, the Grant years merit comparable attention.

Assuming power on the heels of military rule, Grant's presidency marked yet another important phase of Reconstruction. Occupying eight of the period's twelve years, it was the Grant administration that presided over an era of both civil rule and black political power, the existence of which constantly was threatened as an apparatus was built to advance it to new levels. Historians should recognize that the 1870's mark a new phase of presidential Reconstruction, in many ways the polar opposite of Johnson's program. While the seeds of Redemption already were planted in Southern racism before military Reconstruction, the seeds of the twentieth-century civil rights movement were in some sense planted by the realization of the Fourteenth Amendment and the ratification of the Fifteenth Amendment under Grant, which allowed Black Americans a taste of civil and political equality during the nineteenth century.

There can be little question that Grant played a decisive role during Reconstruction. While Congress maintained the initiative until December 1869, Gillette points out that subsequently Grant, "being the first to formulate policy and to take action, had to act in effect as a chief legislator who shaped the law and as a chief justice who interpreted it."[440] He played a major role in securing the Fifteenth Amendment, the Enforcement Acts, and the Civil Rights Act of 1875.[441]

Additionally, black representation rose substantially during the 1870's, and Grant made an unprecedented 249 black appointments during his first term, including foreign ministers, West Point cadets,

---

[439] Current, pp. 4-5.

[440] Gillette, p. 170. Gillette, of course, concludes Grant failed in his task.

[441] As Gillette points out, "Grant most definitely did put his personal stamp of approval or disapproval on a number of federal actions that vitally affected . . . each of the southern states." Ibid., p. 77. See also Boutwell, *Reminiscences* II, pp. 48, 229-30.

customs collectors, postmasters, and tax assessors.[442] More importantly, Grant's dedication to Reconstruction made him a significant moral force. He confronted the realities of racial violence and continued to assert the wisdom of a policy he knew was unpopular. In this sense, he transcended the role of a politician. The subject of mass appeal as a general, Grant the president confronted realities that were perhaps too troubling for a generation of Americans to face that already had witnessed the most radical upheaval in the nation's history.

Gillette's study clings to the idea that federal mismanagement with Grant at the helm was a decisive factor in bringing about the retreat from Reconstruction during the 1870's. The author is never able to explain why he concludes that Grant had a "preference for a passive rather than an active presidency"[443] while observing that "he frequently behaved" to the contrary.[444] He instead concludes, without offering supporting evidence from Grant's own words, that the president "more often than not thought, talked, and acted like an intense factionalist engaged in favoritism, rewarding unreliable friends, punishing honest critics, and stubbornly protecting a discredited regime or an old cohort in trouble."[445] (Hesseltine's pre-revisionist study paints a strikingly similar portrait.) An observation is even reserved for an incongruent picture of Grant in which the "political strengths and weaknesses" of the president "were precisely the opposite of his military strengths and weaknesses."[446] Gillette's account represents an awkward attempt to reconcile many unreliable judgments of the traditional consensus, which ironically were motivated by scholars with diametrically opposed views on Reconstruction, with Reconstruction revisionism. The result reflects the author's bewilderment as he is left to attribute his conclusions on the "paradoxes within his policy"[447] to Grant's "strain of capriciousness."[448]

While he seems to aim for a new interpretation of a series of events that previously has been misunderstood, Gillette ultimately attaches what resembles an old interpretation to events that he characterizes with

---

[442] Foner, pp. 537-38; Sinkler, p. 135.
[443] Gillette, p. 169.
[444] Ibid., p. 173.
[445] Ibid., p. 174.
[446] Ibid., p. 175.
[447] Ibid., p. 173.
[448] Ibid., p. 169.

confusion. Where Grant's intervention in the South was less than a particular governor ultimately requested, as in the case of North Carolina, Gillette tends to view the president as irresolute and disingenuous, despite other factors (such as the unlawful conduct of the Holden government, Republicans believing their own governor deserving of censure, and the clear will of the majority of the state) that urged prudence and restraint.[449] Where Grant took bold action that evoked widespread opposition throughout the country, as with Louisiana and the Civil Rights Act of 1875, Gillette tends to respond with severe criticism that it was a needless drain on his presidency.[450] (Is Gillette suggesting that Grant would have done more for his credibility had he supported the far more dubious cause of Governor Holden?) The author's assessment of Grant's Southern policy is largely confined to regional observations about Southern Republican groups and discussion of the executive and legislative branches almost as if they existed in a vacuum.

In the end, Gillette views Grant's situation as a series of "challenges that required joining bureaucratic expertise and military muscle to political judgment," but in his undeveloped and conclusory argument, he fails to demonstrate a full appreciation of his own phraseology.[451] Apparently overlooking the momentous expansion of federal enforcement power in the birth of the Justice Department and the most extensive peacetime use of troops within the states in history, Gillette underestimates the impact of the most important component of any political situation in the United States: the people. His analysis of Grant's political judgment ignores the extent to which actions he took with regard to the South ran against public opinion—and, in turn, against history. Gillette certainly cites much evidence of the increased public condemnation of federal intervention in the South, but he does not factor it into his negative assessment of Grant, which fails not only because it is counterhistorical—dependent on what might have been— but also because the evidence cited, if anything, supports the opposite of the author's conclusions.

---

[449] Ibid., pp. 94, 174.
[450] Ibid., pp. 134-35, 278-79.
[451] Ibid., p. 185. McFeely reaches a similar conclusion, though in no less speculative form than Gillette. See McFeely, p. 425.

The idea of a thesis that suggests that Grant was an obstacle to Reconstruction's success[452] challenges any sense of historical perspective since commentaries from the 1870's through most of the twentieth century indicate that virtually all condemnation of his Southern policy was motivated by his dedication to it. While there were plenty of contemporaries who came to find Grant a political impediment precisely because of his dedication to Reconstruction, Gillette cites not a single contemporary to support the notion that Reconstruction itself was hindered by the president. Such a thesis also defies the final assessment of Frederick Douglass:

> To [Grant] more than to any other man the negro owes his enfranchisement and the Indian a humane policy. In the matter of the protection of the freedman from violence his moral courage surpassed that of his party; hence his place at its head was given to timid men, and the country was allowed to drift, instead of stemming the current with stalwart arms.[453]

To suggest that Reconstruction might have endured under conditions of civil rule if only Grant had possessed the intangible traits of "a master politician,"[454] despite overwhelming popular judgment to the contrary, asks the reader to accept some extraordinary and unsupported assumptions about the nature of American government. Gillette's study transfers blame from the people to government leaders as the Dunning school had. The author recognizes the racism that afflicted both North and South, but when he turns to an assessment of Grant, this recognition appears to be preempted by criticism based upon the platitudes of the traditional consensus. To whatever extent Gillette and McFeely represent an emerging school of post-revisionist thought based upon

---

[452] Gillette, p. 180. One recent study, apparently working largely from McFeely's innuendos, takes a further step toward distorting Grant's record. Commenting on Grant and the demise of Reconstruction, it states, "Whether he could have reversed this course and finished the business of Reconstruction is doubtful. The point is that he would not try. On a field of battle this human bulldog would not surrender. On matters of race he would not fight." O'Reilly, p. 53. Such a conclusion can come only from a profound misunderstanding of the facts. This is especially unfortunate in view of the study's aim to analyze presidents and racial politics.

[453] Douglass V, p. 202.

[454] Gillette, p. 179.

expectations or disappointments of the late twentieth century,[455] projecting such premises onto the 1870's constitutes a serious loss of historical perspective.

The most significant obstacles to Grant's Southern policy emanated from the will of the people, and a true "master politician" as traditionally understood in American history simply does not jeopardize his power stakes by subjecting himself to a political mine-field without gains that might compensate for injury. The consummate politician might have repeated Lincoln's remark, "My policy is to have no policy,"[456] and allowed Southern politics to take its course as the people overwhelmingly wanted.

Grant did otherwise. He adhered to a policy of intervention when the current of history seemed to dictate the contrary. Gillette criticizes the 1875 Civil Rights Act on the grounds that it "helped bring into power the enemies of reconstruction."[457] From a certain perspective, of course it did. That is what made Reconstruction a catch-22 for Grant: to take action on behalf of Southern blacks during his second term was to invite the nation to amplify its call for a retreat from Reconstruction. The stronger the action, the stronger the reaction.[458] (It thus should not be surprising that the majority-white Southern state in which the Republicans remained in power the longest was Florida, where the relatively non-aggressive Republican regime was atypically unreceptive to the interests of the state's blacks.[459]) By 1876, with Congress, the Supreme Court,[460] and the people having given up on Southern blacks,

---

[455] Foner explains that influential historians who were "[s]hocked by the resistance to racial progress in the 1960s and the deep-seated economic problems the Second Reconstruction failed to solve" depicted change during Reconstruction as "fundamentally 'superficial.'" Foner, p. xxii. A skeptical view of the period was extended to virtually all aspects of Reconstruction in the 1970's and 1980's.

[456] Donald, p. 131.

[457] Gillette, p. 278.

[458] Compare Nevins' suggestion that deprivation of blacks' political power gave rise to greater tranquility: "When Mississippi and Louisiana, Florida and South Carolina were again governed by their own whites, the whole South would enjoy order and a fair degree of racial concord—and not until then." Nevins, p. 740.

[459] Shofner, pp. 38-39.

[460] Interestingly enough, the federal judiciary, which lagged behind both the legislative and executive branches in supporting Reconstruction during the

Reconstruction—and, in turn, enforcement of two major constitutional amendments—were hanging by the thread of presidential support. In 1877, that thread disappeared with the arrival of a new president, and Reconstruction officially ended.

Then again, to frame Grant's task strictly as that of a politician might be as serious a mischaracterization as labelling the Civil War and Reconstruction as exclusively political issues. In many ways, the role of General-President Ulysses S. Grant was not merely that of a politician, but of a revolutionary.

Still, Grant's critics seem to ask, was the president attempting to enforce a revolution for the sake of people or party? Frederick Douglass affirmed Grant's "entire freedom from vulgar prejudice of race and color," and John Mercer Langston concluded that Grant "has showed himself an active, honest advocate of the negro and their friend."[461] Nevertheless, Gillette attributes Grant's actions during Reconstruction to "mixed and obscure" political considerations and cronyism that left the president substantially unconcerned about Southern blacks.[462] Writing before revisionism, Hesseltine views Grant's Southern policy in terms of the president's misguided partisanship (ironically similar to Gillette in many ways). For Hesseltine, Grant's primary concern was the "problem of keeping the South in the Republican ranks . . . ." He supported the enfranchisement of blacks because it "would mean an addition 'to the Union-loving and Union-supporting votes.'"[463] Hesseltine's central conclusion on President Grant asserts, "Although he grew as a President, his growth was that of a party politician. . . . As he acquired the ideology of the politician he lost the vision of the statesman. . . ."[464]

1870's, was the first branch to renew government action on behalf of Southern blacks in the twentieth century. This was possible primarily because the courts were able to utilize the constitutional mandates that still remained from Reconstruction.

[461] Sinkler, p. 151; Simpson, "Butcher?," p. 74. Boutwell also asserted that Grant "was free from race prejudice . . . ." Boutwell, *Reminiscences* II, p. 236. Grant himself once remarked, "I don't know why a black skin may not cover a true heart as well as a white one." Simpson, "Butcher?," p. 74.

[462] Gillette, pp. 79, 167-68. For Gillette's appraisal of Grant's performance, see Chapter 7, "A Study in Incongruities: Grant's Southern Policy and Performance," pp. 166-85.

[463] Hesseltine, pp. 189, 417.

[464] Ibid., p. viii.

This depiction of Grant's attitude raises serious questions about the author's own judgment. His failure to identify Grant's motives and long-term vision of political and civil equality undermines what amounts to his central thesis on Grant as president. "In fact," Benedict asserts, "Grant did seem to perceive himself as a man above parties. He chose his cabinet from among the least partisan . . . of Republicans, so much so that Republicans in Congress rebelled."[465] True, but how did Grant view the relationship between party and Reconstruction issues? Why did the president pursue justice in the South amid opposition of which he was well aware? Did he, as Gillette and Hesseltine continually infer, do so primarily to attain Republican power stakes in the South? In his Sixth Annual Message, the Republican president made a plea that far transcended party:

> Under existing conditions the negro votes the Republican ticket because he knows his friends are of that party. Many a good citizen votes the opposite, not because he agrees with the great principles of state which separate parties, but because, generally, he is opposed to negro rule. This is a most delusive cry. Treat the negro as a citizen and a voter, as he is and must remain, and soon parties will be divided, not on the color line, but on principle.[466]

It is essential to realize how deep the divisions were between the major parties at the time; in fact, party divisions ran no deeper at any time in American history than between the years shortly before and shortly after the Civil War. Despite the professions of the "new departure," the Democratic Party of the Grant era, particularly by virtue of its position among white Southerners, was too deeply entrenched in opposition to the advancement of blacks—and, more dangerously from the standpoint of the former slaves, in an unwillingness to act against racial violence and intimidation—to consider including their interests in its platform.[467] It will be recalled that Grant initially hoped for a conciliatory policy toward the South, but he later commented upon the fundamental issue that made him unwilling to pay the price of conciliation:

---

[465] Benedict, p. 361.
[466] Richardson IX, p. 4253.
[467] Hesseltine, pp. 369-70.

There is nothing more natural than that a President, new to his office, should enter upon a policy of conciliation. . . . I was as anxious for such a policy as Mr. Hayes. There has never been a moment since Lee surrendered that I would not have gone more than half-way to meet the Southern people in a spirit of conciliation. But they have never responded to it. They have not forgotten the war. . . . The pacification of the South rests entirely with the South. I do not see what the North can do that has not been done, unless we surrender the results of the war. I am afraid there is a large party in the North who would do that now. . . . I think Republicans should go as far as possible in conciliation, but not far enough to lose self-respect. Nor can any one who values the freedom of suffrage be satisfied with election results like those in the last canvass for the presidency. . . . Whether it was wise or unwise to have given the negro suffrage, we have done so, and no one can look on satisfied and see it taken from him. *The root of the whole difference lies in that.* [emphasis added][468]

What both Gillette and Hesseltine fail to understand is that Grant's first concern was to preserve those gains for which he had fought so hard during the war; his desire for conciliation was outweighed by deeper values. Grant unquestionably became a firm advocate of the Republican Party, but this was because the Democratic Party failed to depart from a platform he saw as unquestionably antithetical to the cause of the Union, a cause he associated directly with the Thirteenth, Fourteenth, and Fifteenth Amendments:

There is nothing I have longed for so much as a period of repose in our politics, that would make it a matter of indifference to patriotic men which party is in power. I long for that. . . . Before the war, whether a man was Whig or Democrat, he was always for the country. Since the war, the Democratic party has always been against the country. That is the fatal defect in the Democratic organization, and why I would see with alarm its advent to power. . . . *[Behind a Democratic president,] what would you have? . . . the solid South, a South only solid through the disfranchisement of the negroes.* . . . The triumph of a Democratic party as it was before the war, of an opposition party to the Republicans as patriotic as the Democratic party before the war, would be a matter to be viewed with indifference so far as the country is concerned. The triumph of the Democratic party as now organized I would regard as a calamity. I wish it were otherwise. I hope every year to see it otherwise. But as yet I am disappointed. *I am a Republican because I*

---

[468] Young, *Around the World* II, pp. 359-61.

am an American, and because I believe the first duty of an American—
the paramount duty—is to save the results of the war, and save our
credit. [emphasis added][469]

Gillette and Hesseltine confuse the cause and the effect of Grant's partisanship. Grant's loyalty aimed toward securing the gains made during the war; Democratic principles opposed this effort while Republican principles supported it; therefore, his loyalty was with the Republicans. This concurs with the spirit of Grant's other comments on race: for the president, the "prejudice to color" and its manifestations were simply un-American. Grant's motivations as president cannot be isolated from the rest of his career, which bolstered a personal interest in seeing the advancement of the former slaves. For Grant, the suppression of blacks assailed the fruits of the war victory he had

---

[469] Ibid., pp. 268-70. According to Rep. Lynch, Grant described the results of the Civil War in their 1875 conversation as follows:

When the War came to an end it was thought that four things had been brought about and effectually accomplished as a result thereof. They were: first, that slavery had been forever abolished; second, that the indissolubility of the Federal Union had been permanently established and universally recognized; third, that the absolute and independent sovereignty of the several States was a thing of the past; fourth, that a national sovereignty had been at last created and established, resulting in sufficient power being vested in the general government not only to guarantee to every State in the Union a Republican form of government, but to protect, when necessary, the individual citizen of the United States in the exercise and enjoyment of the rights and privileges to which he is entitled under the Constitution and laws of his country. In other words, that there had been created a National citizenship as distinguished from State citizenship, resulting in a paramount allegiance to the United States,—the general Government,—having ample power to protect its own citizens against domestic and personal violence whenever the State in which he may live should fail, refuse, or neglect to do so.

Lynch, pp. 153-54. For Grant, it was clear at that point that "the results of the war of the rebellion" would soon be "in a large measure lost," by which he meant "that the first two of the four propositions above stated will represent all that will have been accomplished as a result of the war, and even they, for the lack of power of enforcement in the general government, will be largely of a negative character." Ibid., p. 155.

forged, not to mention the racial order that he had enforced as general-in-chief during military rule.

Woolley contends that the "soldier's spirit of obedience—unquestioning obedience to law, whatever might be the consequences—was the chief factor in all Grant's dealings with the South during his presidential term."[470] This assessment shortchanges recognition of Grant's role as a legal innovator with heartfelt ambitions for American democracy by overlooking the obvious: it was President Grant who worked enthusiastically to secure the ratification of the Fifteenth Amendment between 1869 and 1870. "Unquestioning obedience" does not innovate the Constitution, and the amendment Grant repeatedly invoked to justify his Southern policy was none other than the amendment he had worked to pass in 1869 while it was a mere proposal without any force of law.

Nevins portrays an incompetent president, "sadly crippled by his total ignorance of law, ... [which] helps to explain Grant's failure in Southern affairs . . . to respect the Anglo-American tradition of the subordination of the military arm to the civil power."[471] Nevins' conclusions reflect the author's own unequivocal, but highly questionable, position-taking, as seen in his blunt charge that a pro-Grant senator was on "the wrong side more often than the right" by virtue of his being, among other things, "a Radical upon Southern Reconstruction" and "a warm supporter of Dominican annexation."[472] From the account that follows Nevins' central conclusion that Fish was "the leader who . . . saved" Grant's "Administration from total disgrace,"[473] the reader is given the impression that the Secretary of State was responsible for virtually every redeeming trait of the Grant presidency (that is, of those few traits that escape Nevins' condemnation). A departure from Dunning would question this portrayal, for Fish was conservative on race issues and tended to counsel against Grant's strong stands in the South. Revisionism additionally overturns Nevins' assertion on Grant's befuddlement with regard to the law.

However, Nevins perhaps unintentionally offers a formidable challenge to any revisionist who believes that Grant remained devoted

---

[470] Woolley, p. 182.
[471] Nevins, p. 134.
[472] Ibid., p. 495.
[473] Ibid., p. vii.

to the political equality of blacks by pointing to an excerpt from Fish's diary in 1877 that would be quoted by several later scholars, including Gillette: "He [the president] says he is opposed to the Fifteenth Amendment and thinks it was a mistake, that it had done the Negro no good, and had been a hindrance to the South, and by no means a political advantage to the North."[474] Considering Grant's expressed enthusiasm in 1870 over the "measure of grander importance than any other one act of the kind from the foundation of our free Government to the present day,"[475] Nevins raises a legitimate issue that has prompted some later historians to draw conclusions implying Grant's racial conservatism or outright hypocrisy! Such historians should realize that Grant's views on the issue did not depart at all from his desire to preserve the civil and political rights that the war had gained for Black Americans. To the contrary, Grant's views at the end of his presidency were quite radical, as seen in his statement less than two years after the 1877 entry in Fish's diary:

> Looking back over the whole policy of reconstruction, it seems to me that the wisest thing would have been to have continued for some time the military rule. . . . Military rule would have been just to all, to the negro who wanted freedom, the white man who wanted protection, the Northern man who wanted Union. . . . I think a mistake was made about suffrage. . . . In giving the South negro suffrage, we have given the old slave-holders forty votes in the electoral college. They keep those votes, but disfranchise the negroes. That is one of the gravest mistakes in the policy of reconstruction. . . . I am clear now that it would have been better for the North to have postponed suffrage, reconstruction, State governments, for ten years, and held the South in a territorial condition. . . . But we made our scheme, and must do what we can with it. Suffrage once given can never be taken away, and all that remains for us now is to make good that gift by protecting those who have received it.[476]

The meaning of Nevins' excerpt appears entirely different in the face of this more thorough explanation of Grant's views. Additionally, Grant seems to have recognized more than later historians the extent to

---

[474] Nevins, p. 853; Gillette, p. 375. Another misinterpretation of this quote can be found in Carpenter, pp. 167-68.
[475] Richardson VIII, p. 4010.
[476] Young, *Around the World* II, pp. 362-63.

which Reconstruction presented political difficulties—perhaps to the point of requiring revolutionary conditions to endure. Putting it simply, Grant observed, "The trouble about military rule in the South was that our people did not like it. It was not in accordance with our institutions."[477] It may have been the case, as post-revisionists in Gillette and McFeely's school do not seem to appreciate, that the most desirable conditions for the continuation of Reconstruction would have required stricter policies than are practicable under conditions of American civil rule.

While Gillette and McFeely, unlike Coolidge, Hesseltine, and Nevins, have the opportunity to reconsider Grant in light of Reconstruction revisionism, they fall short of success, so a reliable, comprehensive evaluation of Grant as president in the context of revisionism has yet to be written. While Grant has been readily associated with a conservative economic tradition by those who condemn it, he is conspicuously absent in references to the "party of Lincoln" by those who attempt to connect the Republican Party to its strong civil rights record in its early history. In truth, Grant more fully embodied what many associate with the term "party of Lincoln" than Lincoln did. For years, the value of Grant's presidency, so deeply connected to Reconstruction, has been swept under the rug along with Reconstruction itself. One sympathetic but apologetic assessment published two years after his presidency seems to recognize this:

> President Grant took his seat in the presidential chair just after the close of one of the most terrible civil wars which ever, with its earthquake throes, agitated any nation. The difficulties which pressed upon him were greater than any of his predecessors had ever encountered. No mortal wisdom could have marked out any measures which would have met with universal approval.
>
> The Southern States were thrown into a chaotic condition. Their peculiar institutions, which had separated them from the North, had perished forever. To make us a homogeneous republic, where *equal rights for all men* should be universally respected, it was needful that several million illiterate slaves, entirely unaccustomed to self-government, should be elevated to the dignity of citizens. This could not be accomplished without great difficulty. It was one of the most perplexing of political problems. When the passions of the present hour shall have passed away, no candid mind will doubt that President Grant,

---

[477] Ibid., p. 363.

embracing in his patriotism all sections of the country alike, has acted in accordance with his most deliberate judgment for the good of all.[478]

When one reads Dunning, Hesseltine, Nevins, Gillette, and McFeely, it is unclear that the passions of the hour ever truly passed away; they seem to linger today, even though the purported basis for them changes.

If Grant were to be carefully considered in the context of Reconstruction revisionism, historian Richard N. Current asserts that his ranking in history would be quite different:

> Grant's low repute among historians has been largely a product of the Dunning school. His fame continues to suffer even though the Dunning interpretation as a whole has long been discredited. It is time that revisionist scholars, having already revised practically every other phase of Reconstruction, should reconsider the role of President Grant.
>
> There can be no doubt that, in the future, he will rank much higher than he has done in the past. If he was not one of the more successful war presidents, he was, in a certain respect, one of the greatest, if not the greatest of all presidents. In this respect, only Lyndon B. Johnson can even be compared with him. None of the others carried on such a determined struggle, against such hopeless odds, to give reality to the Fourteenth and Fifteenth Amendments and to protect all citizens of this country in the exercise of their constitutional rights.[479]

Andrew Johnson and Grant assumed diametrically opposed positions on Reconstruction, and it is ironic that while the Dunning school praised Johnson for defending the Constitution in the face of overwhelming opposition, revisionism ultimately might view Grant in a similar light. While traditional historians have seen in Grant the "puzzled pathos" perceived by James Russell Lowell in 1870, "as of a man with a problem before him of which he does not understand the terms,"[480] it is no inconsequential observation that President Grant's understanding of the most pressing issue of his day outlasted that of both his contemporary enemies and future generations of historians and found new acceptance a century later. One is hard pressed to find another president about whom the same can be said on as central an issue.

---

[478] Abbott, pp. 515-16.
[479] Current, p. 8.
[480] Coolidge, p. 284.

By failing to provide an adequate analysis of the Grant administration, historians have deprived history of one of the most extraordinary (and disturbing) dimensions of the "Second American Revolution"—of the ultimate meaning of the Civil War, of a presidency defying history, of one of the most turbulent chapters in race relations, of unparalleled peacetime challenges to American federalism, and of constitutional innovation followed by decades of perhaps the most blatant disobedience of constitutional amendments in U.S. history. If it could be otherwise, the nation might learn more about itself in both its strengths and its weaknesses.

VI

CONCLUSION

Grant's years in the White House covered a major transition in the history of the nation. Some who mourn the end of the older way of life view the period as a "Tragic Era," and others have seen it as the "Emergence of Modern America." Still others broaden the term "Reconstruction" to apply it to a transformation of the entire national life during the Grant years. "But whatever the name applied," Hesseltine points out, "the facts of transition stand out in bold relief."[481] The Civil War gave rise to what some historians call the "Second American Republic," in many ways a new country in which the preeminence of a national identity and federal sovereignty was firmly established. While Johnson's administration was substantially confined to the task of repairing the damage done during the preceding four years, it was under Grant that national issues and the meaning of leadership assumed a new context, one which would help define modern America. For all this new context is apparently worth, however, President Grant receives little attention, despite the fact that his administration covered some of the first questions that ultimately would determine the position of the United States in the modern world.

More important than the observation that certain issues began to face the country while Grant was president is how he handled them: whether the issue was economic policy, foreign affairs, or civil rights, Grant established a record on the questions he encountered with a decisiveness that towers above the record of other presidents. His stand on monetary policy effected a party realignment and set the stage for

---

[481] Hesseltine, p. 291.

future debate, and his successors through the nineteenth century never achieved their own economic goals as clearly as Grant did through the Resumption Act.   The president's firm stand for peace and the recognition of American interests abroad helped gain the United States unprecedented respect around the world during his presidency, and while the Grant administration reflected the largely isolationist tendencies of the time, in the process of confronting the crises that faced him, Grant played a major role in establishing what would become the motivating principle behind a new world order during the next century.   Grant's record on civil rights stands alone in his era, a fact that is largely intertwined with Reconstruction's repudiation, and even this repudiation could not endure after the government passed measures nine decades later to recover the legal framework of civil rights that had been either created or otherwise realized under Grant.

On other relevant issues, such as the Indian question and civil service reform, Grant played the role of initiator by providing an impetus for the far-reaching changes that were to come in both areas of policy in future decades. The notion that Grant was a president without policies stands in stark contrast to a record that indicates strong leadership (even if that leadership sometimes was manifested in "hidden hands"-style interaction with congressmen). Grant's presidency, which occurred during a period of unprecedented internal growth, which began in the face of so many unanswered political questions, and which ended having answered virtually every question facing it, established the foundations of modern America largely in the same way Washington's presidency shaped the earlier establishment.   Writing from a pre-Reconstruction revisionist perspective, Coolidge asserts, "If we except the baneful Southern problem which was bequeathed to him, and where his fault, if fault there was, lay in the rigid execution of the law, it would be hard to place the finger now on an executive policy approved by him which subsequent experience has condemned."[482]

While historians widely praise James K. Polk for successfully achieving most of his original platform, it is noteworthy that Grant not only fulfilled the commitments he made in his First Inaugural Address,[483] but, unlike Polk, he did so without leaving a legacy that would come to absorb the nation in disaster. At the same time, Grant displayed a flexibility that allowed him to adjust to changing

---

[482] Coolidge, p. 533.
[483] See Richardson VIII, pp. 3960-62.

circumstances. Although he initially expressed his belief that the goal of readmitting Virginia, Mississippi, and Texas into the Union would "thus close the work of reconstruction," he came to see that Reconstruction would require ongoing attention as new challenges were raised, and he adjusted his own course accordingly.[484]

The extent to which historians have displayed confusion over even the basic features of a presidency that contains so many elements of singularity suggests the magnitude of the need for reconsideration. Grant is a president whose appraisal in history requires not merely a more balanced assessment, but a sweeping reexamination from its foundations. However, historians, "following closely in the traditions of Grant's political opponents," have displayed a greater inclination toward keeping "alive much of the partisan criticism of his enemies . . . ."[485] It is the apathy toward substantive considerations that accompanies such an inclination that largely explains how historians could have taken a 180-degree turn in their assessment of Reconstruction, the largest issue that faced President Grant, and still have given him the same condemnatory rank among presidents that he received while the Dunning school prevailed.[486]

A look at all of the pressing issues during the Grant administration, but especially Reconstruction, clearly indicates that the portrait of politics during the 1870's as a mere matter of who practiced a less desirable system of patronage and who advocated civil service reform is not just oversimplified, but distorted. The traditional verdict on the Grant presidency does not even begin to appear logical until one accepts the flawed assumption that the corruption/civil service reform issue was more important than such issues as Reconstruction, international crises, Indian affairs, and the many economic matters the nation faced, all *combined*. After putting the period into perspective and appreciating the gravity of the issues involved, the "history" passed down by Grant's critics reads like the spin of a political faction whose stands on substantive issues are so meritless that it must revert to a focus on the superficial or the false rather than the substance. (Even if its issue emphasis were valid, the traditional consensus' presentation of corruption/civil service reform under Grant distorts a record that actually contains more positive than negative features.) The reformers

---

[484] Ibid., p. 3983; Grant, *Papers* XX, p. 21.
[485] Hesseltine, p. vii.
[486] Murray & Blessing, pp. 16-17.

aimed first and foremost to break the power base of their opponents, and historians have so unquestioningly accepted their premises that they somehow have allowed history to condemn politicians for operating effectively as politicians in the context of their time—which is precisely what the largely out-of-power reformers intended in their own political battle.

Historians' apathy toward studying the pressing (though seemingly bleak) issues of the Grant presidency in the face of more widely studied administrations of lesser consequence to history, combined with the methodologically lopsided nature of the little study that already has taken place on the subject, has helped make existing literature on President Grant collectively one of the most analytically impoverished traditions in the realm of presidential history. This trend can be expected to persist as long as Gilded Age reformers continue to persuade supposedly objective historians to behave like their partisan converts.

It has become fashionable to condemn the Grant presidency and, in terms of a historian's reputation, it is risky to do otherwise. The professionalization of American history has not always made history-writing conducive to the historian's independence, and even a peripheral observation of Henry Adams' commentary indicates that a fair reappraisal of Grant will require historians to overcome the limitations of their own profession. As long as scholars can be expected to fail to transcend the analytical immaturity of the traditional consensus, readers can be expected to enter and exit studies of the Grant presidency without a grasp of the issues involved. While the portrait of a few good men opposing Grant's corrupt party henchmen makes interesting reading, it is one-dimensional and inaccurate, and the Grant presidency covers too many substantive issues to be written as if it were a satire or melodrama.

Also inaccurate is the view that Grant's wartime qualities abandoned him during peacetime. William T. Sherman once asserted that "General Grant more clearly than any other man impersonated the American character of 1861-65."[487] However, Grant's story is one of ongoing growth. The awakening and sharpening of his perception of the issues that faced the country continued after his war career and into his presidency. According to Catton, his entry into the White House was

---

[487] Fuller, p. 94.

tragic "because such a role called on him to transcend the national character; and instead of transcending it he embodied it."[488]   It is precisely this view that fails to take into account the growth of a president who withstood the public clamor for war and encountered political difficulties when he transcended his contemporaries on the era's central issue of American democracy.   It should not take tremendous insight to realize that by 1877, the man who in 1868 had emphasized the importance of the "will of the people" had disappointed expectations that his earlier statements predicted a weak executive who would cave into pressure at the expense of his commitment to the law. Transcendence in Grant's case sometimes has been mistaken for ineptitude by both the president's enemies and historians whose own insight into the period is limited.

However, subjects unjustly evaluated by the historical establishment as unimportant or deserving of condemnation are not necessarily inclined to see a change in status. This dilemma remains unsolved in the case of President Grant. The first step of the solution emerges with the realization that when Richard Hofstadter asserts that "not much need be said" on the Grant presidency,[489] he stands corrected.

---

[488] Catton, p. 134.
[489] Hofstadter, p. 223.

BIBLIOGRAPHY

Abbott, John S.C. *Lives of the Presidents of the United States of America, from Washington to the Present Time.* Boston: B.B. Russell and Co., 1879.

Abels, Jules. *The Truman Scandals.* Chicago: Henry Regnery Co., 1956.

Adams, Henry. *The Education of Henry Adams.* New York: Modern Library, 1918.

Armbruster, Maxim Ethan. *The Presidents of the United States: A New Appraisal from Washington to Kennedy.* New York: Horizon Press, 1963.

Badeau, Adam. *Grant in Peace.* Hartford: S.S. Scranton, 1887.

Bailey, Thomas A. *Presidential Greatness.* New York: Appleton-Century, 1966.

_____. *Presidential Saints and Sinners.* New York: The Free Press, 1981.

Barber, James G. *U.S. Grant: The Man and the Image.* Washington: Smithsonian, 1985.

Barnhart, Michael. "Cabinet All-Stars" in *Newsday*, Dec. 4, 1988, p. 4.

Benedict, Michael Les. "Ulysses S. Grant" in *The American Presidents.* Frank N. Magill, ed. Vol. 2. Passadena: Salem Press, 1989.

Blaine, James G. *Twenty Years of Congress: From Lincoln to Garfield.* 2 vols. Norwich: Henry Bill Publishing Co., 1884.

Boutwell, George S. *The Lawyer, the Statesman, and the Soldier.* New York: D. Appleton and Co., 1887.

_____. *Opinion of Hon. George S. Boutwell upon the Question "Whether W.W. Belknap, the Respondent, is Amenable to Trial by*

Impeachment for Acts Done as Secretary of War, Notwithstanding His Resignation of Said Office." Washington, 1876.

_____. *Reconstruction: Its True Basis.* Boston: Wright and Potter, 1865.

_____. *Reminiscences of Sixty Years in Public Affairs.* 2 vols. New York: McClure, Phillips, and Co., 1902.

Bowers, Claude G. *The Tragic Era: The Revolution after Lincoln.* Cambridge: Houghton Mifflin, 1929.

Boynton, H.V. "The Washington 'Safe Burglary' Conspiracy" in *American Law Review*, vol. 11, no. 3, Apr. 1877, pp. 401-46.

Carpenter, John A. *Ulysses S. Grant.* New York: Twayne Publishing, 1970.

Cashman, Sean Dennis. *America in the Gilded Age.* New York: New York University Press, 1988.

Catton, Bruce. *U.S. Grant and the American Military Tradition.* New York: Grosset and Dunlap, 1954.

Church, William C. *Ulysses S. Grant.* New York: G.P. Putnam's Sons, 1897.

Conkling, Alfred R. *Life and Letters of Roscoe Conkling.* New York: Charles L. Webster, 1889.

Coolidge, Louis A. *Ulysses S. Grant.* Cambridge: Riverside Press, 1922.

Corning, A. Elwood. *Hamilton Fish.* New York: Lanmere Publishing, 1918.

Cross, Nelson. *The Modern Ulysses.* New York: J.S. Redfield, 1872.

Current, Richard N. "President Grant and the Continuing Civil War" in David L. Wilson and John Y. Simon, ed., *Ulysses S. Grant: Essays and Documents.* Carbondale: Southern Illinois University Press, 1981.

Donald, David H. *Lincoln Reconsidered: Essays on the Civil War.* New York: Vintage Books, 1961.

Douglass, Frederick. *The Frederick Douglass Papers.* 5 vols. New Haven: Yale University Press, 1979-1992.

DuBois, W.E.B. *Black Reconstruction.* New York: Harcourt, Brace, and Co., 1935.

Dunning, William Archibald. *Reconstruction: Political and Economic.* New York: Harper and Brothers, 1907.

Fish, Carl Russell. "*Ulysses S. Grant.* By Louis Coolidge" (book review) in *American Historical Review*, vol. 22, pp. 885-86 (1917).

Foner, Eric. *Reconstruction: The Unfinished Revolution, 1863-1877*. New York: Harper and Row, 1983.

Franklin, John Hope. *Reconstruction: After the Civil War*. Chicago: University of Chicago Press, 1961.

Fredman, Irwin F. "The Presidential Follies" in *American Heritage*, vol. 38, no. 6, Sept./Oct. 1987, pp. 38-43.

Fuller, J.F.C. *Grant and Lee: A Study in Personality and Generalship*. Bloomington: Indiana University Press, 1957.

Garfield, James A. *The Diary of James A. Garfield*. Vol. 3. Harry James Brown and Frederick D. Williams, ed. East Lansing: Michigan State University Press, 1967-1981.

Garland, Hamlin. *Ulysses S. Grant: His Life and Character*. New York: Macmillan, 1898.

George, Mary Karl. *Zachariah Chandler: A Political Biography*. East Lansing: Michigan State University Press, 1969.

Gillette, William. *Retreat from Reconstruction, 1869-1879*. Baton Rouge: Louisiana State University Press, 1979.

Grant, Jesse R. *In the Days of My Father General Grant*. New York: Harper and Brothers, 1925.

Grant, Julia D. *The Personal Memoirs of Julia Dent Grant*. John Y. Simon, ed. Carbondale: Southern Illinois University Press, 1975.

Grant, Ulysses S. *Conversations and Unpublished Letters*. Michael J. Cramer, ed. New York: Eaton and Mains, 1897.

_____. *General Grant's Letters to a Friend, 1861-1880*. New York: T.Y. Crowell and Co., 1887.

_____. *The Papers of Ulysses S. Grant*. John Y. Simon, ed. 20 vols. to date. Carbondale and Edwardsville: Southern Illinois University Press, 1967-1995.

_____. *Personal Memoirs of U.S. Grant*. 2 vols. New York: Charles L. Webster, 1885.

Harris, William C. *The Day of the Carpetbagger: Republican Reconstruction in Mississippi*. Baton Rouge: Louisiana State University Press, 1979.

Hesseltine, William B. *Ulysses S. Grant: Politician*. New York: Dodd, Mead and Co., 1935.

Hoar, George F. *Autobiography of Seventy Years*. 2 vols. New York: Charles Scribner's Sons, 1903.

Hofstadter, Richard. *The American Political Tradition*. New York: Vintage, 1989.

Hoogenboom, Ari. *Outlawing the Spoils: A History of the Civil Service Reform Movement, 1865-1883*. Urbana: University of Illinois Press, 1961.

"Impoundment" in *American Heritage*, vol. 25, no. 1, Dec. 1973, pp. 22-23.

Jackson, Carlton. *Presidential Vetoes, 1792-1945*. Athens: University of Georgia Press, 1967.

Jones, James Pickett. *John A. Logan: Stalwart Republican from Illinois*. Tallahassee: University Presses of Florida, 1982.

Jordan, David M. *Roscoe Conkling of New York: Voice in the Senate*. Ithaca: Cornell University Press, 1971.

Keller, Robert H. *American Protestantism and United States Indian Policy, 1869-82*. Lincoln: University of Nebraska Press, 1983.

Ketcham, Ralph. *Presidents Above Party*. Chapel Hill: University of North Carolina Press, 1984.

Key, V.O. *Southern Politics in State and Nation*. New York: Vintage Books, 1949.

Library of Congress. Ulysses S. Grant Papers.

Logan, Mary. *Reminiscences of the Civil War and Reconstruction*. George Worthington Adams, ed. Carbondale and Edwardsville: Southern Illinois University Press, 1970.

Lynch, John R. *The Facts of Reconstruction*. New York: Arno Press and the New York Times, 1968.

Magrath, C. Peter. *Morrison R. Waite: The Triumph of Character*. New York: Macmillan, 1963.

McFeely, William S. *Grant: A Biography*. New York: Norton, 1981.

McPherson, James. *"Grant: A Biography*. By William S. McFeely" (book review) in *Civil War History*, vol. 27, no. 4, Dec. 1981, pp. 362-66.

Milkis, Sidney M. and Michael Nelson. *The American Presidency: Origins and Development, 1776-1990*. Washington: Congressional Quarterly, 1990.

Morgan, H. Wayne, ed. *The Gilded Age: A Reappraisal*. Syracuse: Syracuse University Press, 1963.

Murray, Robert K. and Tim H. Blessing. *Greatness in the White House*. 2nd ed. University Park: Pennsylvania State University Press, 1994.

The Nation.

Nevins, Allan. *Hamilton Fish: The Inner History of the Grant Administration.* New York: Dodd, Mead, and Co., 1936.

New York Times.

New York Tribune.

Novick, Peter. *That Noble Dream: The "Objectivity Question" and the American Historical Profession.* Cambridge: Cambridge University Press, 1988.

Official Proceedings of the Republican National Conventions of 1868, 1872, 1876, and 1880. Minnesota: Charles W. Johnson, 1903.

O'Reilly, Kenneth. *Nixon's Piano: Presidents and Racial Politics from Washington to Clinton.* New York: The Free Press, 1995.

"Overrated and Underrated Americans" in *American Heritage*, vol. 39, no. 5, July/Aug. 1988, pp. 48-63.

Pierce, Edward L. *Memoir and Letters of Charles Sumner.* 4 vols. New York: Arno Press and the New York Times, 1969.

Polakoff, Edward L. *The Politics of Inertia: The Election of 1876 and the End of Reconstruction.* Baton Rouge: Louisiana State University Press, 1973.

Porter, Horace. *Campaigning with Grant.* New York: Century, 1897.

Proceedings of the Senate sitting for the trial of William W. Belknap, late Secretary of War, on the articles of impeachment exhibited by the House of Representatives. Forty-Fourth Congress, First Session. Washington: Government Printing Office, 1876.

Rejai, Mostafa and Kay Phillips. *Demythologizing an Elite: American Presidents in Empirical, Comparative, and Historical Perspective.* Westpoint, CT: Praeger, 1993.

"Resumption of Specie Payments," in *Appleton's Annual Cyclopædia and Register of Important Events of the Year 1879.* New York: Appleton and Co., 1880.

Richardson, James D., ed., *Messages and Papers of the Presidents.* Vols. 8 and 9. New York: Bureau of National Literature, 1897.

Ross, Ishbel. *The General's Wife.* New York: Dodd, Mead, 1959.

Rossiter, Clinton. "The Presidents and the Presidency" in *American Heritage*, vol. 7, no. 3, Apr. 1956, pp. 28-33, 94-95.

Rushmore, Elsie Mitchell. *The Indian Policy during Grant's Administrations.* New York: Marion Press, 1914.

Scaturro, Frank. *The* Alabama *Claims, the Treaty of Washington, and the Establishment of the Principle of International Arbitration.* Unpublished paper on file with author, 1996.

Schurz, Carl. *The Reminiscences of Carl Schurz*. Vol. 3. New York: The McClure Co., 1908.

Senate Library. *Presidential Vetoes, 1789-1988*. Washington: Government Printing Office, 1992.

Sherman, John. *Recollections of Forty Years in the House, Senate, and Cabinet*. 2 vols. Chicago: Werner Co., 1895.

Shofner, Jerrel H. "Florida: A Failure of Moderate Republicanism" in *Reconstruction and Redemption in the South*. Otto H. Olsen, ed. Baton Rouge: Louisiana State University Press, 1980.

Simon, John Y. "Preface to Second Edition" in Matthew Arnold, *General Grant*. Kent, OH: Kent State University Press, 1995.

Simpson, Brooks D. "Butcher? Racist? An Examination of William S. McFeely's *Grant: A Biography*" in *Civil War History*, vol. 33, no. 1, 1987, pp. 63-83.

_____. *Let Us Have Peace: Ulysses S. Grant and the Politics of War and Reconstruction, 1861-1868*. Chapel Hill: University of North Carolina Press, 1991.

_____. Letter to Frank Scaturro, August 1991.

_____. "Ulysses S. Grant and the Electoral Crisis of 1876-77" in *Hayes Historical Journal*, vol. 11, Winter 1992, pp. 5-22.

_____. "Ulysses S. Grant and the Failure of Reconciliation" in *Illinois Historical Journal*, vol. 81, Winter 1988, pp. 269-82.

Sinkler, George. *The Racial Attitudes of American Presidents: From Abraham Lincoln to Theodore Roosevelt*. New York: Doubleday, 1971.

Smith, Theodore Clarke, *The Life and Letters of James Abram Garfield*. 2 vols. New Haven: Yale University Press, 1925.

Sproat, John G. *"The Best Men": Liberal Reformers in the Gilded Age*. New York: Oxford University Press, 1968.

Storey, Moorfield and Edward W. Emerson. *Ebenezer Rockwood Hoar: A Memoir*. Boston: Houghton Mifflin, 1911.

Taylor, Tim. *The Book of Presidents*. New York: Arno Press, 1972.

"The Ten Best Secretaries of State—and the Five Worst" in *American Heritage*, vol. 33, no. 1, Dec. 1981, pp. 78-79.

Testimony Taken by the Joint Select Committee to Inquire into the Condition of Affairs in the Late Insurrectionary States: South Carolina. 3 vols. Washington: Government Printing Office, 1872.

Tugwell, Rexford G. *How They Became President: Thirty-Five Ways to the White House*. New York: Simon and Schuster, 1964.

Ulysses S. Grant Association brochures through 1995.

United States Reports (abbreviated U.S.). See individual cites.

Webb, Ross A. *Benjamin Helm Bristow: Border State Politician.* Lexington: University Press of Kentucky, 1969.

White, Leonard D. *The Republican Era, 1869-1901.* New York: The MacMillan Co., 1958.

Williams, Charles R., ed., *Diary and Letters of Rutherford Birchard Hayes.* 5 vols. Columbus: Ohio State Archaeological and Historical Society, 1922.

Wilson, James G. *Life of John A. Rawlins.* New York: Neale Publishing Co., 1916.

Wise, John S. *Recollections of Thirteen Presidents.* New York: Doubleday, Page, 1906.

Wister, Owen. *Ulysses S. Grant.* Boston: Small, Maynard, and Co., 1901.

Woodward, C. Vann. "The Lowest Ebb" in *American Heritage*, vol. 8, no. 3, Apr. 1957, pp. 52-57, 106-09.

Woodward, W.E. *Meet General Grant.* New York: Horace Liveright, 1928.

Woolley, Edwin C. "Grant's Southern Policy" in *Studies in Southern History and Politics.* Inscribed to William Archibald Dunning. New York: Columbia University Press, 1914.

Young, John Russell. *Around the World with General Grant.* 2 vols. New York: American News Co., 1879.

_____. *Men and Memories: Personal Reminiscences.* 2 vols. New York: F. Tennyson Neely, 1901.

INDEX